Huncke

A Poem & Paintings

By

Rick Mullin

EXOT BOOKS
NEW YORK

www.exotbooks.com

Second Edition, Revised
Copyright 2021 EXOT BOOKS
All Rights Reserved
Typeset in Marion and Attic Antiqua
ISBN: 978-0-9898984-5-4

Design: Julio M. Perea

Acknowledgments

The author would like to express gratitude to the following whose help and guidance were essential to the first and second editions of *Huncke*:

David Lawton (master of ceremonies), Sarah Lundberg (reception), Quincy R. Lehr (evangelist), Marybeth Rua Larson (friend and critic), Dr. Whupass (gray eminence), Alicia E. Stallings (advice to "Keep going" after reading the first canto at Eratosphere), Eratosphere (the living university of music theory), Don Zirilli (who opined), John J. Trause (advocate), Stephen Wesche, (inside photos), Peter Jacobs (cover photos), Benjamin Franklin ("scientist, jounalist, and [wow!] inventor"), Penn Yan (portage), John Marcus Powell (seen in basement on the night in question), Thurston Moore (strange licks), Rose Kelleher (likes), Maryann Corbett (measures), Robert Olen Butler (first thought, best thought), Mike Alexander (male model), Brooklyn (sunrise), New Jersey (sunset), Lincoln (tunnel), Exot (last exit).

Contents

Why A Redux		XVI
Canto One	An Invitation	1
Canto Two	The Night Begins	5
Canto Three	Oklahoma	11
Canto Four	New York	17
Canto Five	The Onyx	25
Intermezzo	Part One — Trenton	33
Intermezzo	Part Two — Mischianza	39
Canto Six	The Studio of Probst	45
Canto Seven	Beat	55
Canto Eight	The Couch	65
Canto Nine	The Rape of Manhattan	71
Canto Ten	Finale	83
Lost Canto	The Wilderness	89

Rick Mullin's Huncke
    By Paul Christian Stevens   **101**

Betcha Can't Read It Just Once
    By Siham Karami   **109**

Paintings

Portrait of Paul Weingarten	IV
Portrait of David Lawton	XXII
3 O'Clock, Hoboken Station	4
Kinsale Man (Portrait of Brendan Egan)	10
East River	16
Parker	24
George Washington after a Portrait by an Itinerant Portraitist	32
Benjamin Franklin after a Portrait by an Unknown Painter	38
Lois, Portrait of the Artist's Mother	44
Paul Weingarten with a book on Van Gogh	54
Detainee	64
Giuliani in Times Square, or The Rape of Manhattan	70
Figure (Night Class Model)	82
Abraham Lincoln	88
Paul Stevens	100
Siham Karami	108
Self Portrait	114

Cover: Portrait of Paul Weingarten (detail)
Back cover: Self Portrait, Beat (detail)

Huncke: A Poem
in its second edition
is dedicated to

Sarah Sunflower Lundberg

who shared my admiration for the paintings of Jack Yeats
and whose enthusiasm for this project
threw a rainbow of gasoline
over a tentative but determined flame.

Why a Redux?

Once, on YouTube, I saw a video of the night in question. In it, I can be seen for a split second standing alone in a crowd of people in the basement of a club called Bowery Electric. Other videos taken that night, including a pretty good one of Patti Smith playing guitar and reciting poetry on stage, are easy to find. But the one I remember with me in it for a moment seems to have appeared and disappeared, much like the book I wrote inspired by the event, and very like its hero.

That gathering, a tribute reading for the Beat progenitor Herbert Huncke, took place eleven years ago. The following year my book, *Huncke*, a 10-canto poem with two intermezzos written in ottava rima, was published in Ireland, of all places. Significantly, I am holding a pint of Guinness Stout as I flash in and out of the lost basement video. Maybe 30 copies of the book were sold before its publisher went out of business. I am told that its inventory was pulped, but I can't verify anything beyond the book's appearance and disappearance.

I have one or two copies of *Huncke*. If I had more, I would probably pulp them too. I can't look at it, which is perhaps a healthy predicament for a writer in regard to his or her debut volume—*Straight ahead!* In my case, there is the added aversion to a slew of editing errors that prompted the publisher to offer a corrected second edition shortly before its demise some years back. I might have taken them up on it. Now it seems I have.

On its tenth anniversary, it occurred to me that *Huncke* might have something to say in this strange new decade. The Great Recession of 2008 figured prominently in the first edition of *Huncke*. The economy rebounded, but the heartland did not. Human dignity from Western Pennsylvania to Bakersfield, California, is at low ebb. America is drugged out, thanks to a healthcare system corrupt to the point where serious people are howling for an American brand of socialism. The table seemed set for a reread, which inevitably resulted in a redo.

Thus, the second edition of *Huncke* is a reconsideration. Many of the stanzas have been improved with care taken to keep the original narrative on track. That narrative, which uses Herbert Huncke as a scaffold for a gloss on American social issues, art, and history, has been extended with the "discovery" of a lost canto. "The Wilderness" stands as a kind of correction in that any gloss on American history should probably touch on the Civil War.

It also adds the perspective of ten more years of American history: protracted war and the advent of President Donald Trump; the further division of society into red and blue camps increasingly biased toward narrow, media-defined perspectives, increasingly hateful of each other; the rise of Black Lives Matter and *@MeToo*, pointing to an intensification of perennial race and gender equity issues, a pandemic, and a political landscape such as we have not witnessed in 52 years. The net effect is a kind of creeping numbness as the inconceivable becomes profane fact. Sometimes it seems that all we can do to get at the truth is to communicate our experience, to imagine the divine. To create. So, I'll give *Huncke* another go.

Art played a part in the first edition, which was illustrated with sketches by Paul Weingarten, whose landscape painting of a Queens power station landed on the cover. The new edition is illustrated by my own paintings, including portraits of Weingarten, and one of David Lawton who co-hosted the Huncke reading at Bowery Electric. Lawton, the dedicatee of the first edition, serves as the model for the Poet Morton in *Huncke*. I have broken my severe edict against painting from photographs for portraits of Lincoln and Charlie Parker, both of whom feature prominently in cantos of the poem. I also cheated in this regard with portraits of two poets and critics I admire: Siham Karami, who contributed an essay, and the late Paul Christian Stevens, whose review of *Huncke* in *The Shit Creek Review* in 2010 appears in this new edition. Many thanks to them.

And thanks to R. Nemo Hill and Julio M. Perea, the co-editors of Exot Books who agreed that a second edition of *Huncke* was in order and who, sending me back to the easel more than once, produced a beautiful, carefully edited and curated volume.

Thanks also to those who read, and especially to those who *re-*read, *Huncke*. Such readers may well be poets themselves. All honor is due to them, which I suppose is the purpose of this book. I offer it with thanks and praise to the Bowery ghosts and angels playing the networks of America at night, and to the city, or what's left of it, leaning on its river into yet another day.

Rick Mullin
Feburary 2021

The eyes open to a cry of pulleys,
And spirited from sleep, the astounded soul
Hangs for a moment bodiless and simple
As false dawn.
        Outside the open window
The morning air is all awash with angels.

                      Richard Wilbur
                      Love Calls Us to the Things of This World

Canto One

An Invitation

I'm swallowed by the room in Morton's eye.

I

The poet Morton from the open mic
invited me on Facebook to a bar.
A night of poetry. It meant a hike
down Bowery, but it wasn't all that far—
he'd organized the reading, and I like
the guy, despite the skulls on his guitar
and his "Memorial for Herbert Huncke,"
the prototype for William Burroughs' Junkie.

II

He'd signed on Thurston Moore from Sonic Youth
and Patti Smith; some doyennes of the scene
who carried less marquee. To tell the truth,
he'd resurrected quite the old routine
of Squeaky Frommes with little John Wilkes Booth.
I'd never been particularly keen
on hipster scribblers, but, you see, I'd sent
out invitations to my own event...

III

and so I went. To Wikipedia
to bone up on the luminary thief
and prostitute, whose online media
runs viral with a hypertext relief
that lights full paragraphs. Review procedure:
Click the automatic links for brief
biographies that conjure a penumbra
of young ambitious writers at Columbia.

IV

But here's the nut. He grew up middle class,
he ran away, and lived through the Depression
hobo style. In time, he worked his ass
on 42nd Street and took confession
from the Ginsberg lot, who paid in grass.
Suburban junkies followed in succession.
He held court at the Chelsea in his bed—
the tab was covered by the Grateful Dead,

V

and that was that. And this is Houston Street
and Bowery- "Bumland!" (Lots of kids from Jersey
smoking cigarettes outside effete
cafés and bars). I feel I'm at the mercy
of nostalgia, marching to the beat
of hand-me-down catastrophes and hearsay
revolutions in the spoken word
toward some theater of the absurd,

VI

where, down the stairs in the performance space,
I see a flock I flew with years ago.
I smile at every bright, familiar face
I pass. I sip a beer. A vertigo
ensues in which projected figures race
through shadows, cycling to a garish glow.
I'm swallowed by the room in Morton's eye.
If Byron needs a hero, so do I!

Canto Two

The Night Begins

I opt to persevere, now I've begun.

I
I opt to persevere, now I've begun.
My hope, to plumb the alternate dimension
I described as arcing from the sun
in Morton's solar system. My intention—
reportage. Indulge me if I run
the gamut such that anyone's attention
span is taxed, if any episode
proliferates or breaks a fire code.

II
For that's the nature of the pilgrim's tale,
and certainly the Poet Morton's night
of ardent readings in memorial
will conjure pilgrims, honoring their plight
and plaintiff maunderings. A setting sail
across America's agenda. Right?
I don't think we can put a timer on it.
This isn't going to be another sonnet.

III
The introductory palaver wraps
as Morton pans the crowd for Reader 1.
A hand goes up and everybody claps.
Get ready for a shot of beatnik fun
and games! Perhaps berets and finger snaps.
And bongos... Dobie Gillis, anyone?
OK. Let's leave the attitude behind.
Approach the evening with an open mind.

IV
Think nothing if the light resolves to scenes
on Rampart Street, the far end of the Quarter.
We knew we'd get the bit on New Orleans,
and maybe from a fallen actor's daughter—
but Tatum is a no-show. So the beans
and rice are parted from the muddy water
by a cat called Moses and his mix
of hat and scarf and tablet politics.

V

A reading from *The Herbert Huncke Reader*:
We're taken to a joint called Alcazar
where Huncke meets a grifter. Call him Peter.
They're leaning on a shaky plywood bar,
the three-time loser and the bit repeater.
There's talk about a dancer and a jar
of whiskey. "Man, she goes down on a dollar."
Huncke's game: "Let's give the girl a holler!"

VI

The scene that follows, utterly profane
with vicious slurs and racial epithets,
is hardly worth recounting: Sugar Cane
and *Chocolat*, most dismal of vignettes.
And here we're grinning, listening again,
the poet Morton calling in all bets
as brother Moses, to the manor born,
heads up the 'Ssippi, blowin' on a horn.

VII

O Delta Jazz! O bottled switchyard red
that leads to Sterno squeezed through a bandanna!
O vision of the hero getting head.
O peeling of the narrative banana.
The outlaw ambling, crawling through a dead
end district hoping for one more *mañana*,
living it, vicarious, for you.
The quiet desperation. Working blue.

VIII

How often have we heard America
extol such rugged individuals
with river song? Sweet esoterica
is ready-made, like the residuals
from straight talk customers' satirical
encounters with the devil. Pity fools
who haven't got Old Red Foot on the run.
Bring on the Bell, the Bible, and the Gun.

IX

But aren't there also secret dining halls,
the Skull and Bones® and ivy-covered bricks?
Societies behind the climbing walls
and benches of Phi Beta Kappa® pricks?
And are these not the guys who roll the balls,
and isn't it about fraternal tricks?
Of course it is! A little game sequestered
from all the big sky traffic moving westward.

X

Head west across the Delaware. You'll see
a sign that reads: *America Starts Here!*
It rambles on to Sacramento, free
and brave, but takes a little detour near
Columbus to avoid Chicago—*Ski
the Poconos!* and *Have Another Beer!*—
the billboards foliating fore and aft,
and every Huckleberry has his raft.

XI

But don't forget the crossing headed *east*
to Trenton on that freezing Christmas day,
the interruption of an English feast
where pints of Hessian beer were put away.
It wasn't viewed as Hoyle in the least.
An indolent dragoon was heard to say,
"These blokes are quite more bother than the Scots!"
An angel in the whirlwind called the shots

XII

and hovered in that smoky coffee house
in Philadelphia. We see a clutch
of Masons in the corner and a mouse
in close confabulation. Double Dutch
is called outside the window as a souse
stands up to toast an act of treason such
that brother Mick, the rodent, perks his ears
and, snapping a suspender, hollers, "Cheers!"

XIII

A shrill falsetto. Everybody laughs.
But in a room upstairs, another story
edges sideways, adding to the gaffs
we cherish in recorded history:
John Adams, with impromptu epigraphs,
implores his bedmate, Franklin, that he's "sorry,"
but he needs the window closed. "What's more,
methinks there be guerrillas! Bar the door!"

XIV

Still, "mouse" will out! Slips Mickey through the cracks
to mount his own campaign at riverside,
a boatman in the artery that tracks
its course down center to the wafting tide
of mediocrity and fame. Relax.
There's money in it yet!... Yes, let it slide.
We haven't seen the last of treasonous
itinerants or "Steamboats" squeezin' us.

XV

And let us not exchange mythologies
but hold our own and press them to the vest,
abjuring others'. No apologies
for this! The poet Morton can attest
to the importance of ontologies
and subterfuge, avoiding an arrest
in matters of a logos at the bottom
of a river. Smoke 'em if you got 'em.

Canto Three

Oklahoma

America was dying. So were we.

I
The Hero. There's a hand we over-play.
Byronic, comic, cult, and existential.
Cowl and cape. A vapid sobriquet
suggesting *Good v. Evil* in sequential
pen strokes and balloons. An overlay
of black on white. Let's stick to the essential
grey—and light it with the kind of fire
that rugged individuals admire.

II
And drop the politics, for Jesus sake.
It mixes with the arts the way that rock
gets on with scissors—scissors tend to break.
Of course there's always paper, which is stock
to fuel the fire drum. But I should take
a little breather on this circuit, hock
the saxophone, and head out on the rails.
The narrator defers to pilgrim tales.

III
Our second reader ambles to the stage—
a heavy, white-haired stevedore adjusts
his glasses and the microphone. A page
slips sideways, animated, riding gusts
of stage draft to his boots. (The wind doth rage
and crack its cheeks!) He clears his throat and trusts
in all that Eastside worker sympathy.
And, thus, appearance is reality.

IV
"What else is there to work with?" Huncke asks.
An ashen dustbowl in the fading sun,
the fossil flatland Oklahoma masks
its own potential energy. A run
of iron underground and over tracks,
an exothermic culture where the gun
suggests another iron line that turns
to crumpled newsprint. "Anything that burns!"

V
Regarding headlines: *Nobody is Hiring*.
An Oklahoma of the unemployed,
he thinks. A range where nobody is firing
the heirloom arms—(though cops have long enjoyed
a cushion of security). Retiring
with the embers, Huncke views destroyed
horizon east- and westward and a rail out
of a landscape hungry for a bail-out.

VI
This he rides at sunrise on the blind.
A journey toward an easterly injection
where vermillion hits the ground, a kind
of natural narcotic or reflection
of a bleeding eye on Paradise, resigned
to moaning low and missing its connection.
Like missing breakfast on a boxcar floor?
Here's Huncke, quoted by our stevedore:

VII
"America was dying. So were we.
We understood that any meal we shared
at railyard rendezvous could damn well be
our last. We learned to trust. Oh, we were scared,
but we devised a brotherhood with three
things needed to survive—a heart prepared
to *not* survive, a ready case of lies,
and skill at knowing liars by their eyes.

VIII
And so, with elemental grunts and stares,
we treated friend and enemy alike
through latent afternoons. We heard the prayers
of proselytizing strangers on the pike.
Some radical ideas. But workers' cares
were not exactly resonating. Strike
or no, our raps were non-deferrable,
though railyard skills would prove transferable."

IX

An interview with Dr. Kinsey, next:
"So, tell me more of what went on in jail."
"...I thought your questions had to do with sex!"
"I'm getting there." "The bastards read our mail.
So we devised a code. An oral text
of silence called *The Order of the Rail.*"
"...That's it? You know I'm paying you for this."
"Hey I'll be back. I gotta take a piss."

X

It's funny how so little said can say
so much and launch a literary style.
And how that style, sufficient to the day,
repeats itself. How sometimes angels smile.
The stone is struck just right and sparks the way
that Kerouac lit up a country mile.
The way that certain predecessors did:
Somewhere a cop is beating up a kid.

XI

...*And I'll be there!* But I should act my age.
For now, I'll leave you with the picture of
that fallen sheet of paper on the stage.
Regard its blankness, whiter than a dove.
But don't forget the fire in its cage!
It isn't garbage that I'm thinking of,
but energy, potential, under stress.
I owe it to America, I guess.

Canto Four

New York

Brooklyn spikes vermillion light quite early with the dawn.

I

The poet Morton sat out Canto Three,
but he was busy with the clipboard, pal.
The man behind the curtain took a knee.
His Bluetooth kept him linked to the corral
of readers in the Green Room, to the free
association. And his ear canal
was buzzing. Oh, he didn't miss a beat.
And Lo! The poet Morton's on his feet!

II

Full-bounding like Colossus to the mic,
a Jason having bagged his Golden Fleece.
Like Patton's Seventh Army on a hike,
he slams the music stand and hollers, *"Peace!"*
The audience reaction? Zombie-like.
He thunders through his introductories,
And, coming off a bit like Mickey Rourke,
he sings of the arrival in New York...

III

of Herbert Huncke: Eighth and 42.
The photograph is largely black and white
but Kodachrome is making its debut.
He wears a boutonnière for Friday night,
a zoot suit and an alligator shoe.
A panatela waiting for a light
hangs fires through the air of Morton's tale,
a token of *The Order of the Rail.*

IV

The Horn & Hardart won't let Huncke in:
Our hero telegraphs a latent danger.
Sunken charcoal eyes and jaundiced skin—
the pancake make-up marks him for a stranger.
It vectors him. A city where the sin
of loneliness is mortal cannot change her
rules with every landfall from the bus.
The lonely men call, "Buddy, you're with us!"

V

He works the matinees and small hotels,
developing a habit and a barter
system. Hearing the cathedral bells
reminds him of Chicago. He's a starter
and a finisher who'll push it if it sells—
a lady client keeps him at The Carter.
In Oklahoma, Huncke was the payer.
On 42nd Street, they'll call him Mayor.

VI

It all goes well, until there comes a war,
requiring him to work another angle.
The Red Hook sunrise spikes the lower jaw
of Brooklyn, and the day becomes a tangle
with the law of averages—the corps
are shipping overseas. We hear him jangle
pennies in an empty movie house.
Eventually, he falls in with a mouse,

VII

 that pencil scratch we last saw leaving Philly
doing business on the maritime
in Hollywood—a.k.a. Steamboat Willie.
The portent of another life of crime
for Huncke, Mickey Mouse did not look silly
leaning on the wheel. He looked sublime!
There's something about a rodent when he whistles
that calls up better days and guided missiles.

VIII

"Hey, look! That's Roosevelt and Einstein, Mick!"
The newsreels interrupt the broad cartoons,
though lines are often blurry—it's a trick
they play in theaters. And the balloons
go up: *"I know these guys,"* the chirpy prick
conveys. *"They're amateurs. Two more buffoons
who still refuse to see the bigger picture."*
Now Mickey slips through an ungodly stricture.

IX

"There're little cracks in everything," laments
the lonely prostitute. "And walls
to hold 'em up." There's whistling in the vents
and heating pipes of dingy hotel halls,
but little action. Negative events
bring Huncke to a place where he recalls
a vision of his hero as a sailor.
He goes around the corner to his tailor.

X

We cut to Normandy. It's quiet now.
The bodies of Americans rise up
and fall like Ahab's arm. And how
they beckon as we fail to measure up
the depths they tumbled from the sunken prow
or from the tearing cumuli. A cup
of sand per pint of blood. A caput mortuum.
America fell hard across the fulcrum.

XI

It happened yesterday. A dollar short
and roughly halfway through the century,
a merchant mariner, his first report
"in theater," arrives today to see
the furrows on the smoking beach. His port
of call a ceaseless howl. The memory
will track him through a constant alleyway.
A funnel of the dead. A passion play.

XII

For weeks he falters on the broken coast
of France. The poet Morton speculates
(for Huncke leaves us on the beach) that most
of what the sailor passes percolates
subconsciously. It's woven in a host
of anecdotes about New York or states
out west. The clues are there. But if you miss them,
our hero's open to the barter system.

XIII

It's Thomas Pynchon, I believe, who wrote
about the chronic yo-yoing persona
extant in the Navy. I should quote
the passage. But, instead, a brisk hosanna
to the recluse will suffice. A pea coat,
yes—the merchant type. But I am on a
stanza clock, so if it's all the same,
I'll just say Huncke sails to whence he came.

XIV

At Sea: The sailor tries to keep it clean—
a quite effective means of kicking it.
Despondence holds no sway with our Marine—
"I kept a razor in my sock and quit
the things I couldn't get. The magazines,
the first-run cinema. But there was shit
onboard. Like hits of morphine in syrettes.
I paid the medic off with cigarettes."

XV

Returning to New York and shifting gears,
he decommissions. But he keeps the suit
(he'll wears it through the Eisenhower years)
and stumbles on a famous photo shoot,
The Sailor's Kiss. You'll notice he appears
along the margin on the right. His boot
is bulging just below the whatcha-call-it,
the bulge about the size of someone's wallet.

XVI

And a kid's been trailing him all afternoon.
A schoolboy in a Catholic uniform
whose head looks like a carnival balloon—
it's prematurely balding. Not the norm
for even Catholic tikes. Well, pretty soon
the punk is offering a light. Reform
school etiquette—the contrasts are uncanny.
"So, what's your name, kid?" "Rudy Giuliani."

XVII

[Narrator]: *Now hold it, Morton, you just jumped the shark!*

[Morton]: Not me! I'm reading Huncke from the stone.

[N]: *The future mayor? Midtown, after dark,*
a ten-year-old with matches, all alone?...
Unlikely, bro!...

[M]:   Who led us through the park
in Canto Two?

[N]:   *...Proceed.*

                    ...An ice cream cone
is shared. "So, listen, kid. What's in the box?"
"A mouse. You're gonna love the way he talks."

XVIII

The image on the cardboard lid is rich:
A sailor boy and his demented dog
bust smiling through a drumhead. *"There's* a switch!
What happened to the cartoon pig?!" A cog
and mental flywheel variously twitch,
connecting entries in the seaman's log.
"Not interested, kid. I know its kind.
I'd just as soon ride this one on the blind."

XIX

Their futures fork into the city night.
Young Rudy with his shoebox waddles west,
as Huncke yo-yos east and dogs it right
to 9th. That's all, for now. But you can rest
assured that Brooklyn spikes vermillion light
quite early with the dawn. As Morton's best
performance fades to black, perhaps you're listening.
You'll hear the Buster Brown box, pal. It's whistling.

Canto Five

Onyx

Yardbird goes up flirtin' with the angels.

I

The angels, during inter-canto, smoke
and gossip blithely in the underworld.
The smoke is overpowering there. They choke.
Some rifle through their purses for their pearl
itinerary casebooks as they joke
about their overworld routines. They hurl
their cigs into the tar and hitch their cleats
as sunlight hits the Greenwich Village streets,

II

where snow has fallen overnight. The gutter
catches shards of Brooklyn windows, pink
reflected light that flares until the Cutter
of the Crystal throws it in the sink.
The irretrievability is utter,
like sugar in the coffee that we drink.
Some yo-yos, pal, do not come back around—
There are fundamental changes on the ground.

III

In drugstore windows, television sets
appear with telescoping bug antennae.
There's better living, too, now bigger bets
are down on chemistry. The Injun penny
someone offered for your thoughts regrets
its new trajectory—it hasn't any
choice. The money drops, you hear it clink.
Now you will pay to find out what you think—

IV

the tenet of a prank fraternity
religion. And America's receptive!
Beyond the fulcrum to eternity,
the frontmen of a shadowy collective
cast the logos in modernity
and varnish it with urethane, reflective.
They sell it through those glossy magazines.
Or better yet, it moves on TV screens.

V

"The Rexall store will never be the same!"
That's Reader 4, an artist, sweet and light.
She's pencil thin. Montana is her name.
Ostensibly, she lived through black and white
and knew the corner store. Perhaps I'd frame
it this way: Pushing 60 in a tight
black leotard, her *bona fides* exude
an archetype, experienced and shrewd.

VI

She speaks of solid and ethereal
connections, nets of carbon, silicon
and Space Age Polymer material;
performances at Shea and Budokan,
assassinations, breakfast cereal;
the social views of every pillock on
the radio and other media.
From telegraph to Wikipedia.

VII

Her canvas is a comprehensive stretch
across a framework of conspiracies
we've heard a thousand times before. *Kuh-vetch,
kuh-vetch.* Like other recent centuries,
the twentieth, America's, will catch
the kind of hell in written histories
that reads like *deja vu.* A reckless caper,
typed in pixels, printed out on paper.

VIII

But through the vapid lunacy cuts jazz,
the rhythm and the melody and math,
medieval in a balance that it has
of mind and soul. A sonic polymath
of points in time. Montana's za-zu-zazz
has settled on the scene, the righteous path
of gangster pinstripes, yellow ties, and sound.
Of changes in the air and on the ground:

IX

We sip Manhattans, she and I, OK?
I'm at a corner table with Montana.
We're at The Onyx—Billie Holiday
is on a juke box with the *Vox humana*.
The scene is slipping further into play
(O peeling of the narrative banana)
revealing Baron Rothschild's seventh daughter:
My date's Pannonica de Koenigswarter!

X

Her Mata Hari leg beneath the table
nudges mine. She points her Lucky Strike
directly at the stage, on which a stable
ring of spheres converges on the mic.
The trumpeter, bereted, seems somehow able
to manipulate the atmosphere. I like
his glasses, smile and suit. Hey, Nica, is he...
"Sit down, would you, dear? You're buggin' Dizzy."

XI

The Baroness de Koenigswarter, *née*
Montana, hooks Gillespie's eye. He winks
and lifts his bended horn as if to play.
She lifts her fluted cocktail glass and drinks.
We're filming black and white: her tresses grey,
her features sharp—a veritable minx.
There's something gently tapping on the floor
and quite a big commotion at the door.

XII

The saxophonist, twenty minutes late,
is navigating underworld obstructions
as he rumbles to the stage. Negate
that attitude on temporal reductions!
Time is *change* within the steady state.
The leader makes with truncate introductions:
"Max at bat! I'm blowin' in the cone!
That's Cholly Pock-a-roony on the 'phone,

XIII

Red *Gar*land on the keys! We'd like to ride
a number called *The Order of the Rail*—
a *zip*-bop a-*doo* an' ..." I've never *heard* this side.
At any rate, they blow beyond the pale!
It's *Groovin' High* on *Marmaduke*. A tide
of rising sound, obsession and the Whale.
It's *Ko-Ko* with a dizzy attitude,
a *Steeple Chase* across the latitude

XIV

and long! Hey, there are moments when I'm certain
Dizzy rides an inch above the stage
as little Max creates a weather curtain.
Garland cuts a chord and whacks the cage
from which the flying Yardbird goes up flirtin'
with the Angels. Keep it on the page?
A'right. I do get busy with the phonics.
(But that's the way they blew it at the Onyx.)

XV

They wrap the set and Dizzy hits the gait,
surveying regulars about the room—
"Hey, Dr. Kinsey! Thursday night at 8?
You got it, baby." Then, as you'd assume,
he joins us at the table. "Am I late?"
Now here come Parker, Red, and Max— ka-*zoom!*
into the introduct'ries. *Where y'at?*
...Call me Ishmael. *We can get with that!*

XVI

What *was* that tune? "The missing cut," says Max.
"A sore spot, if you wanna know the truth.
We'd laid it down to take it to the wax,
but monkeys in the back recording booth
kept trippin' on the hot side of the jacks."
I turn to Parker, sipping his vermouth.
—That flew the way of *Donna Lee*, but faster!
"...Some greysuit at Savoy erased the master."

XVII

There follows discourse on the number's theme
and conversation angles like the bell
on Dizzy's horn: the brotherhood, the dream,
the alleys, desolate. The prison cell.
Respect for space, but none for the regime
of frontmen lampin' at the big hotel.
"I guess it's kinda like a *guy*quest, huh?"
"You gonna be like that, Pannonica?"

XVIII

Discussion rattles, spins, and cracks apart.
The topics range from politics to cars,
photography and baseball, modern art,
and cabalist fraternities. And Mars.
Then Red taps Max, "Hey, listen Bonaparte,
I'm noticing more greysuits at the bars."
"Monopolizing Miles's telephone?"
"I notice they prefer to drink alone."

XIX

The drummer's hip to threatening syndicates,
it seems, but bothered by a more direct
concern—the passage of the drummers' kits
through Southern clubs and Northern disrespect.
He's holding photographs. In one he sits
and glowers at a counter. I reflect
on this, look forward to the famous session.
Another sidebar—check out this digression:

XX

"Diz, where's Dexter?" "Gordon? He's in jail!
He's gotta lay off jackin' Buicks, Bird."
"He's gotta kick *The Order of the Rail!*"
"Oh-ho! Now look who's talking, Parker" "...Word."
Gillespie's digs could almost make the sale,
but Bird is clearly slipping. "Bird, I heard
the marshals took him downtown with some junkie."
"...I *told* him 'bout that motherfucker Huncke."

XXI

Pannonica will take him home again,
and Bird will crash and likely stay alive.
But, still, the night is young at half past ten.
The hallowed riffs and conversation thrive
for hours, kind of ebb and flow, but then
it drops. Red Garland calls the place a dive:
"You know a joint is really on the skids
when they start servin' wine to mice and kids."

XXII

...Oh Jesus Christ. That's Rudy Giuliani
in the corner. Nica shakes her head.
"The two of them are regulars. With any
luck, the mouse will pick a fight." Instead,
the cartoon and the fascist swallow many
glasses of a better switchyard red.
"No stopping them," says Max. "And it's a pity.
Those two are gonna move on New York City."

XXIII

The canto's cast and crew now pass before us
knocking over cymbals and a fan.
Archangels, jazzers, grey men in fedoras,
the Beatles on their first tour of Japan.
The waiters at the Onyx, who ignore us.
Montana takes a bow. Go hit the can
or grab another beer. You have permission.

                              We'll have a fifteen-minute intermission.

Intermezzo

Part One
Trenton

And Washington is evidently pissed.

I

We follow bloody footprints in the snow
to find December's general. The camps
along the Delaware are dark below
a shrouded quarter moon. So, tea and stamps
have come to Christmas and a fatal flow
of minor icebergs over Hessian lamps
that glisten in a crooked constellation.
To Pennsylvania's risky debarkation.

II

And Washington is evidently pissed.
(That's Major Wilkinson delivering
a letter). "Why on earth does Gates insist
on penning missives *now?*" The shivering,
exhausted messenger on horseback, fists
in pockets, shrugs. His horse is quivering.
Our general's convinced of his decision.
Still, Philly filibusters for revision.

III

And there are handbills in the bivouacs
entitled *Crisis*. The latest thing from Paine,
the errant pamphleteer who fills the stacks
at better coffee houses with a sane
and measured call to duty and attacks
on George the Third. His broadsides would explain
the mechanisms of our wars to come.
It's said he authored *Crisis* on a drum.

IV

These are the times that try men's souls. That's quite
a memorable line of type. We tucked
it in at school. But think about this night—
the Continental Army truly fucked,
its numbers down, yet bucking up to fight
an empire on the skids... it could get bucked
itself. *The sunshine patriot will shrink
in crisis,* Paine insists. "These things could sink!"—

V

A freezing *midnight* patriot inspects
the barges carrying the heavy guns.
Forget about the painting that reflects
a taste for showboat at the Met—the tons
of metal and the ice each scow deflects
are shadows in a mist that hides the sons
of farmers turned, in crisis, to guerrillas,
tucked into the strangest of flotillas.

VI

At six foot five, three hundred fifty pounds,
that's Henry Knox commanding Coal Barge One,
a persevering Golem. Now he sounds
the general advance, and pushes gun
and gunman from the Pennsylvanian grounds
into the frigid Delaware. The sun
and seated angels wait upon this tower
of a man—it takes about an hour

VII

getting into Jersey. And not without event—
a lot of soldiers fell into the water
more than once as Wilkinson was sent
to Congress with a blank response. His order:
"Give this envelope to Gates." He went.
And then the stolid face upon the quarter
gazed across the unforgiving moat,
a face among some twenty on a boat.

VIII

I've heard it said the Hessians weren't drunk,
and that their fighting socks were pulled up straight.
But I prefer the antique myth. Debunk
away. I have them sleeping with the gate
wide open, rebel columns up the trunk
and in. A shootout in the Garden State
ensues. The turn-around does not take long.
Lieutenant Springsteen puts it in a song:

IX

What is it with the Wars o' Nations,
In 'n' out-type situations
    Bleaker than the Pennsylvania coal.

And what about this State o' Jersey?
Jesus Christ and Lord have mercy,
    Talk about yer fire in the hole!

X

"That's insubordination, but it rocks."
Thus speaks the veritable Frankenstein,
and leader of the river crossing, Knox.
"Ahr vee schtill gettink pait fuhr zis ting?" "...Nein."
As Frankenstein and Springsteen dry their socks,
two Hessians contemplate the *Ausverein*.
And fortune's turnpike bends as fate demands—
now Philadelphia is changing hands.

Intermezzo

Part Two
Mischianza

A glowing Franklin swings on glass harmonic.

I

We're settled in. Just look at Washington
ensconced at Morristown behind the Watchung
Ridge. It's really rather Poshington—
we stroll the public square, and there we watch young
lawyers eat their lunches, talking Toshington.
And tradesmen—here comes Dr. Hu-Wa Chung
the acupuncturist. Hey, where's the pain?
(This town will one day show up for McCain.)

II

But Philadelphia's a contradiction.
On the one hand: Cradle of democracy
where geniuses hold forth in lofty diction.
On the other: Meritocracy
of British military predilection
where Democrats are in the stocks. You see,
King George's boys go quick to kicking asses—
they wouldn't go and hit a guy with *glasses*!

III

Like Franklin. *There's* a city luminary.
A scientist, a journalist, and (wow!)
inventor. Here he's wiring a canary
cage (...we'll... ask him later). Anyhow,
he's off to meet that ship from Londonderry
with the Union Jack tattooed across its prow,
aboard which Joseph Priestley makes his crossing.
It's moored at Philly, finished with its tossing.

IV

A phony beard and hat for a disguise,
our Benjamin, who's now *persona non-*,
is mixing with the turncoats and the guys
in red, a yo-yo-like phenomenon,
he wanders up the dock and down. His eyes,
behind that strange bifocal optikon,
are panning for a kindred soul in *Science*,
that second front in Franklin's rank defiance.

V

"Well met!" and *"Hail!"* and *"Watch yer dobber, pal!"*
The geniuses connect and sally forth
upon the *laboratoire de naturale*,
into a steady headwind from the north.
The doctor's duffle bag bumps into all
the Chestnut Street pedestrians. It's worth
our while at this point to reflect upon
the prior findings of a paragon

VI

of British chemistry, the gaseous sort,
who commandeered the element tagged "O"
and filed a highly referenced report
with *British Chemo Letters.* Even though
that august, grey, and scholarly cohort
of editors were loath to let it go—
an academic quibble, God forfend—
sheer brilliance conquered envy in the end.

VII

I wouldn't call him "Renaissance," no he
is more "Medieval Man"—a theologian
and a scientist, the world of chemistry
his playground into which a sordid Trojan
Horse of inside operatives found entry
as he labored on his anti co-gen
system: gas from captive kilowatts.
Oh, academe has "haves" and "have-it-nots"

VIII

and they'd have none of it. Despite his papers
on the dephlogisticated air
he'd bottled (soda water), and his capers
at the cutting edge in gases, there
were men in the establishment whose tapers
burned at driving Priestley to despair:
"His findings contradict our Institution
of The Light—our Chemo-Revolution!"

IX
So Priestley joined a real one overseas.
Yes. Having failed to disavow the Spirit,
hearing angels blowing in the trees
and saying so to those who wouldn't hear it,
confronting nature sometimes on his knees,
Joe Priestley got the boot. "I do not fear it!"
Priestley wrote with true alacrity.
"I know a guy with electricity

X
emblazoned at the top of his CV,
whose frolics in the field strike me as sound!"
They are indeed. Now in the basement he
and Franklin, hooked up to a proper ground,
will dephlogisticate with gases free
and bottled. Priestley sings. And with a round-
about progression to the supertonic,
a glowing Franklin swings on glass harmonic.

XI
But joy's eclipsed by racket in the streets
as Britain's Howe kicks off the Mischianza
marking his retirement. *"Ze fleets*
ahr out und flying up full-belly an za
Delavare!" von Knypenhausen bleats,
that Hessian drunk. I'll need another stanza
to convey, in faith, the full proportion
of this party and the full distortion

XII
of divined reality attending it.
Three thousand guineas to the outhouse, pal,
with jousting knights along a conduit
of redcoat ranks, a hoop-skirt carnival
and masquerade ball. Sort of ending it,
a fireworks display and bacchanal
that goes on through the Pennsylvania night.
And in the muddy Pennsylvania light

XIII

of dawn, the Mischianza Day Parade
is lining up on South Street, set to go!
There'll be another day of this charade.
Our coverage continues. You should know,
though, of a new technology and trade,
a new direction for the wind to blow—
a guild that calls itself a "Corporation"
advancing via wicked machination:

XIV

Cracked Air Chemicals Incorporated,
Allentown, a manufacturer
of gas, was formed by an excoriated
flank of Freemasons—a fracturer
of air into the free and floriated
ranks of elements. In fact we are
familiar with the science and its source—
See *British Chemo Letters, IX*, of course.

XV

They introduce a "float" at the event,
a canvas sack that shocks von Knypenhaus,
a twisted, levitating shank of tent.
"Mein Gott in Himmel! Die fliegende Maus!
The day, in fact the very air is rent
as General Howe and Hessians *Lauf drauß.*
And Priestley begs, "Ben, say it isn't so."
"I think we're looking at the future, Joe."

Canto Six

The Studio of Probst

Gloria is still inclined to blame herself.

I

Who's that, Huncke moving down the hall?
A little early for the fire escape.
And icy too. *Be careful you don't fall
into that garbage in the alley!* Cape
and cowl? Some counterculture folderol.
Ain't easy getting Huncke into shape.
And harder yet to wrestle with a ghost
who rises with the dawn to rob his host.

II

"That motherfucker Huncke." Gloria
is still inclined to blame herself. Tonight
she shuttled downtown from Astoria
to read her own account, an erudite
depiction of the sanatoria
that laced Manhattan, sheltering the bright
insomniacs—the open-door apartments
of the 1950s. Shared compartments

III

for the flopping souls of college friends
and sailors met at bars. A hardwood tooled
for transience, a long-term residence
for some, these networked urban hovels pooled
a generation searching for a sense
of true community. Each flat was ruled
by some beneficent Victoria.
And such, apparently, was Gloria:

IV

"Your little buddy cleaned us out, Montaigne."
She kicks a lump of sailcloth on the floor.
"Man overboard!" the lump replies. Remain
at ease. The ample snoring hump, ashore
and AWOL, will arise and will maintain
an aura of detachment, and, what's more,
explain the Riot Act before we're read it.
"It's resurrection time, Montaigne." "You said it!"

V

In twenty winks, the Maxwell House is drunk
and Gloria's beneath the waterproof
of Montaigne's pea coat. This deflects a chunk
of ice that plummets from a 9th Street roof.
Now Montaigne pulls his hostess closer. "Junk
will do that to ya, Gloria." Aloof,
yet nestled to the philosophic swab,
she listens once again. "A man will rob

VI

his brother for a fix. His mother too.
In fact some mothers have been known to steal
from churches. *And* their sons. But..." "Listen, you.
We've covered this before. Your little spiel?—
I've memorized it. And I know it's true
that even guys like Huncke..." "...have a keel!
And sometimes friends must help them keep it even."
"Take the tiller...?" "Seein' is believin'!"

VII

Yes, Bob Montaigne had truly straightened up,
with no small thanks to Gloria's ministrations.
No longer wine, but coffee in his cup,
his mind meanders through the variations
on a twist in time, a giddiyap
through Western history. His disputations
seem auricular. Spectacular
his permutations in vernacular.

VIII

By noon, the search for Huncke has become
a cozy walk up Broadway to The Strand.
A bulging pea coat, crewmates on the bum
across the Greenwich Village Winterland.
"I think I'm losing feeling in this thumb."
"Oh, that I were a glove upon that hand!"
"You kill me when you wax all Montaguic...."
"Hey, buddy girl, do I see Jackson's Buick?"

IX
He does. On University, of course.
The Cedar Tavern regulars are holding
forth on abstract painting with the force
of gallery and critic smug and scolding
in their favor. "Granting a divorce
to Universal Truths," Montaigne, unfolding
Gloria into the bar, is heard
to mutter in his scarf, *"The Painted Word!"*

X
For Bob knew Jackson Pollock long before
the galleries, when Jackson had some chops,
before the Greenberg gang could find the door.
But soon enough, the scribblers pulled the stops
on how *"the modernists must guard the store
from capitalist kitsch!"* As one shoe drops
its doppelganger tends to get untied—
now Jackson's gone onto the other side.

XI
"Glad tidings, Pollock, Marko and de Kooning!"
"It's Bob Montaigne, a sailor of the seas!"
"You all know Gloria." "Have we been spooning?"
queries Rothko. Gloria answers, "Please..."
"A Shirley Temple for the sailor!" Tuning
for the metaphysical debate and tease,
de Kooning throws the Shirley Temple punch.
"Be seated, won't you? Jackson's buying lunch."

XII
"But I'm not biting on that flat-out plane
of color. Sorry kids. I want a ducky
or a horse." "A realist! Well, that explains
the hat and pipe." "Say, Bill, today's your lucky
day! For this is *not* a pipe." "Bo'Swain,
you mock me!" "With a mirror to your plucky
movements, right?" The two of them go at it
Greco-Roman style 'til Rothko's had it.

XIII

But clearly talk has tumbled here for hours
with Elaine and Lee and all the Riverside
cotillion at the bar, the Modern towers
and spikes of taste arrayed for regicide.
De Kooning wonders where to send the flowers.
The theory dribbles into the applied,
and since she has the money and the time,
it's body paint for Peggy Guggenheim!

XIV

They have her on the table and have-at
with cans of oily, colored goo. A fling!
And Guggenheim is A-OK with that.
The New York School is on its feet. They sing:
Oh Jackson, Honey, you are where it's at!
"SO HOW COME NO ONE'S BUYING ANYTHING?"
He grabs his hat and stumbles to his car.
"Turn not from gloomy madness in this bar!"—

XV

—a hellish bellow from the snowblind street,
where stands an artist from the neighborhood.
He grimaces and rocks upon his feet,
an Albert Pinkham Ryder beard, a rude
and spattered vest—a painter, indiscreet,
unfettered, and exhausted. "You be good,"
Montaigne shouts to the Cedarites and leaves,
upholding Gloria in pea coat eaves.

XVI

The poet Morton, interlocutor,
steps in to back up Gloria onstage.
"That painter's Joachim Probst," he shouts. And sure
enough, that old reactionary rage
is manifest upon the cellar floor.
"The Jesus painter?!" "Put him in a cage!"
The hipsters boo, grey eminences hiss—
"No worries, Morton. I can handle this."

XVII

Returning to that snowy afternoon
beneath her codependent sailor's wing,
our reader sets about to change the tune
of bigots in the audience who cling
to post-war prejudice and the cartoon-
like compartmentalized re-reckoning
of art. She skewers the phony nomenclature
that cordons paint and poetry from nature.

XVIII

"But, wha'do I know?" Montaigne's favorite question.
Let's send it up, an allegoric cloud
with signage countermanding the suggestion
that *another* critics' camp should crowd
onto the field of theory. Indigestion
can't be cured with *more*. Still, we're allowed
opinions with occasional reversals.
Perhaps it's best to stick to universals.

XIX

"Behold the man!" Montaigne exclaims. "And follow
him!" But it ain't easy running in
another sailor's coat, as through the shallow
slush and deep they go. *"Devout in sin,
have art!, spake Satan. Sing thee Christ and swallow
woe, for woe is will!"* quoth Probst. "Tack in!"
screams Gloria. (The truck says Ballantine).
Familiar streets run somehow labyrinthine.

XX

It must be noted here, Montaigne and "Jack"
had long established a rapport of psalms,
arcane, chaotic, dark.... It dated back
to when Probst's canvases, stigmatic palms
they seemed, debuted on cluttered wall and rack
at the emporia downtown. "My qualms
with all his blatant Christian images
were insignificant. His scrimmages

XXI
with the eternal are what count," Montaigne
explained when Jack once landed on their floor—
the painter left abruptly in the rain
next morning, pausing briefly at their door:
"Come visit at my studio." The pain
that twisted on his bearded face was more
than Gloria could handle at the time—
a Titian graced with Dostoevsky's crime.

XXII
"Today's the day," Bob whispered to the head
against his breast. "I want to see it too,"
said Gloria. "But has he even said
a word to *us?*" "Good question." It was true
that Probst would walk the street and chant his dread
and cryptic catechism to the blue
between the rooftops. "Do you think he sees us?"
"Thou wast the host, now know the host of Jesus!"

XXIII
"...We're in!" They stifle shouts. And now the lights
and shadows on the stage adjust to cast
a lake's late aura dying into night's
as Gloria, a woman with a past
so rich in other people's lives, recites
an ersatz prayer, the sense of which will last
in language not much longer than the taint
of shade along the beach. They watch him paint

XXIV
in semidarkness. It appears the only
source of light comes from the painting, from
within. Indeed, he labors in a lonely
space. It is a blessing to succumb
to such an utter loneliness. "You told me
once that in this city where we come
and go through architecture, very few
will ever find their home." "And if they do,"

XXV

says Gloria, "they live in it alone."
"That's very beautiful." The dying Christ,
a bearded bull in crusted flesh and bone,
in whorls of oil color brushed and sliced
across the canvas, beckons. He is shown
three quarters as a haggard poltergeist,
a father/son act hammered to a tree,
encrypted in a gross androgyny.

XXVI

"The *Bull Madonna Christ* it shall be called."
The artist stakes his reverential claim
before an image horribly recalled
yet purely beatific in its "frame"—
his pictures are most powerful when walled
still warm and very wet among the same
stalactites of the artist's pentiment
that permeate his cracking tenement.

XXVII

Along the floriated walls are stacked
the documents of a prophetic vision.
Congresses of angels, portraits hacked
into impasto fields with light precision
by a hammer blow. A colored tract
on raptured spirits leans on the incision
of a face into the stone ethereal:
The Poet as the Angel Gabriel.

XXVIII

"Is he asleep?" "Or something," says Montaigne.
They check for breathing and they bid farewell
to Probst, the artist who is called "insane"
around the corner at the private well
of the abstractionists. The "madman" in the rain.
We've had a walkthrough at the sleeper cell
and witnessed a medieval sanity,
a window on our dark humanity.

XXIX

And now the burning coals are on the river
to the west—New Jersey in the gloaming.
The crewmates walk in silence with a shiver
now and then beneath the felt. A homing
instinct runs the neighborhood, forgiving
trespasses another penchant roaming
through these streets adjacent to desire,
beneath the smoke of alley cans afire.

XXX

Does Gloria's smile convey a sense of loss?
Compassion as she folds her notebook closed?
An Emma Goldman bowing in the gloss
and glimmer of a Bowery hole, transposed
against a dying image on a cross,
The Rank Homunculus, she has exposed
the audience to an unattended truth.
Next up is Thurston Moore from Sonic Youth.

Canto Seven

Beat

"Am I dreaming?"

I

The kid from Sonic Youth, now 52,
is tall and thin as ever with the wall
of bangs across his eyes. But wouldn't you
expect a "pro" to have the wherewithal
to pace his *Lives of Saints* recital? True,
his rock routines are avant-garde and all—
of course he's gonna don the cowl and cape.
Let's see if we can get his tale in shape.

II

We manage to make out this rare vignette:
a psychiatric ward across the river
in New Jersey—butt of comics, yet
a landscape that has managed to deliver
unto literature a coronet
of poets fortified in mind and liver.
Some names from Paterson? If you insist.
There's Williams...and our next protagonist.

III

"Um, lights out, Ginsberg. Flashlights too."
"I'm sorry Dr. Kinsey. Just a minute.
But...you do night rounds? Really! Good for you."
"You bet your bottom line. There's money in it.
Hey, look. We're human beings. Take a few
and I'll check back." "As gentle as the linnet.
A trait suggesting, well... perhaps suggestions."
"Til then." "Just don't get mental with the questions."

IV

The in-and-out, as always, Kinsey leaves
the patient with a manuscript beneath
a tent of bedding. "Honor among thieves,"
it reads, "a code of conduct to bequeath
unto a generation rolling sleeves
and on the road." The poet picks his teeth.
This needs an awful lot of work, he thinks.
The Order of the Rail...?
                       "That title stinks!"—

V

Another audible hallucination?
Like the one that seemed to be the voice
of God? A deep and sonorous oration.
But that was only William Blake: *"Rejoice!*
O golden Calyx, nail thy dissertation
to the sky!" Well, if he had a choice,
he'd nail it to the bursar and salute.
Columbia had given him the boot.

VI

The verdict on the title is his own.
But Burroughs isn't married to it. No,
the author seemed distracted when he'd shown
this work to Ginsberg. Dazed. But, even so,
compelled to let the better poet hone
the maniac epistle, his tableau
of drifting through the city and the sticks
in search of *virtù* and an angry fix.

VII

"Hey, Solomon, I think I've got a hit
for your old man," says Ginsberg, "but it needs
a little...copy editing and shit."
The sullen gentleman whose hair recedes
the next bed over also studied Lit.
His father puts out paperbacks. "It bleeds
and pukes in places. Marvelous," says Ginz.
Whereat a bend in literature begins.

VIII

And Huncke's bumming on the ride. Ironic,
given that the thieving ectoplasm
hardly measures up to the Miltonic.
Despite the obvious enthusiasm
of our reader, Thurston Moore from Sonic
Youth, the Huncke oeuvre's more phantasm
than phenomenon. Let's not be baffled.
The man is, more than anything, a scaffold.

IX

Yes, narratives in nature coalesce
(a kind of structural biology)
around the junkie. Burroughs's success,
like Ginsberg's, thrives on the rheology
of crime, societal taboo, and stress—
the vagaries of pharmacology.
In this way Huncke serves us as a host
to poets. As a kind of holy ghost.

X

"Injectable!" adds Burroughs, who will share
the sundry laboratory lore and field
experiments in *Naked Lunch*. But where
we have him now is Mexico, a peeled
banana. He becomes a writer there.
Though certain crucial documents are sealed,
his seminal *roman* is fully vetted—
and several readers may have even read it.

XI

Let's not be coy—as everybody knows,
he shot Joan Vollmer in the head. His wife!
A drunken game of William Tell: "Compose
yourself, my love. This kind of shot is rife
with possibilities." "And I suppose
the wineglass is a metaphor for life?"
"Perhaps a thought balloon for guided missiles!"
His brother finds, and bribes, the right officials.

XII

But as we case the scene that prompted Bill
to act upon his literary calling,
it's worth remembering that Huncke still
recalls *his* time with Joan. The two were falling
for amphetamine. The "pilot's pill,"
as it's been called. Now everybody's hauling
ass across the border. All bets are off
on reinterpreting Raskolnikov.

XIII

The poet Ginsberg has his memories
and dreams of Joan. "Can you love your mortal
friends?" he asks her under garden trees
that end up shadowing her grave. "A portal
to the world of darkness might reprise
the light. What follows? Is it love?" A chortle
as the bullet hole and brow bestow
the comfort of a stone in Mexico.

XIV

Or else they ask how Kerouac is doing
(the puncture wound converses on her head
in Dada dream effect). "Well, Jack's pursuing
his satori, digging gold from lead."
"Retailored tailors blush at the ensuing
alterations." "*That* is what *he* said."
"And what of Burroughs?" "Now he writes to save
himself." "The fugitive becomes a slave."

XV

The labial stigmata of the dream,
or *rictus craniale*, if you prefer,
is one of many visions in a stream.
No wonder Blake taps Ginsberg to confer
upon a mystic or romantic theme
from time to time. Again, the liquid blur
of cloud is consecrating Ginsberg's space.
The ward becomes a graphic interface.

XVI

No Blake this time, nor even Father Walt.
The Eisenhower era, black and white
and jittery, submerged below a vault
of winter sky, a trestle, and a flight
of stairs, finds Ginsberg bearing bread and salt.
The Jewish poet, Harlem acolyte,
his matins rang the Ironbound in Newark.
Above his head, the windshield of a Buick

XVII

vaults across the clouds, a silver screen
behind a veil of bathhouse steam and coal.
The firmament is barreling between
the projects on the L.I.E.—the soul
of young America can still be seen
behind the wheel, which is to say, in whole
or part, on Earth and in the busy street,
a naked angel, supplicant and beat.

XVIII

With snow, disaster trees, and faster drivers
cracking through the air, the poet finds
constituents of Genius in its diverse
attitudes about the city. Minds
attuned to jazz, the alien survivors
find their purgatory riding blinds
and walking in a mist of flannel grey,
through charcoal lines sufficient to the day.

IXX

"It's sketchy, but I do make out a scheme,"
sings Ginsberg. "Gadgetry no longer hidden
makes its way up Lexington to ream
the orifice of human soul. Forbidden
light, intelligence, and ardor scream
beneath the rigging of a profit-ridden
engine (Moloch!) in the stark alliance:
Government—meet Industry and Science!"

XX

The ghost in the machine (see title page)
is just around the corner. Leave him there.
His mechanism is the hemorrhage.
He bleeds into the scene. He's no Voltaire,
but the Enlightenment and golden age
beatitudes, the poems and the prayer
to come, will bear his stamp. Defining "Beat,"
the prostitute enables the conceit.

XXI
Well, that speaks to the pudding. Where's the proof?
"It's dragged and dragging through the Negro street,"
to paraphrase The Poem. From a roof,
a radio howls constellations—the elite,
dispersed in asphalt courts and alleys, hoof
kinetic theories in a patterned heat
across a circuit imperceptible
to all but those who are susceptible:

XXII
"We know the Pentagon is in on this.
What isn't clear is how the suits arrange
the game. Now, Ginsberg, you're the Communis'.
Got anything?" "Ah, Neal, you have a strange
and irresponsible hypothesis.
I'm really not a Red!" "But that could change,"
says Huncke, hanging with the High Sephardim.
Says Kerouac, "I think we'll have to card him."

XXIII
This kind of teasing often makes the rounds
among the poets in McCarthyite
America. But Cassady makes sounds
in much the way the radio tonight
produces jazz: *"Not guilty on the grounds
of Rockland!"* "Rub it in, O recondite
and beautiful," replies the Jersey poet.
"I count on your apostasies." "I know it."

XXIV
Above this crooked Barrio, a line
in ultraviolet/black is drawn. The hue
divides the duotone. "A telling sign!
A corporal illumination true
to life," the poet sighs, as Ballantine
in golden neon lends its colors too.
The tri-part basics mix and multiply.
There's elemental change across the sky

XXV

as Ginsberg schleps his sack of salt and bread
to San Francisco (still hallucinating
in the dull infirmary). His head
is bigger now. It's balding and inflating.
He assumes the lotus pose in bed
and chants the Maha Mantra, compensating
for his westerly coordinates,
as does a congress of subordinates.

XXVI

Imagine Ginsberg's head upon a coin.
Or printed on the new-style purple five.
Or might the cosmic eye our bills adjoin
to pyramids be Ginz's? We arrive
at perspectival quandaries and purloin
a cultural prerogative, then drive
it to the blue Embarcadero screaming.
This head grows hard to handle. "Am I dreaming?"

XXVII

Yes or no, he's on the No. 6
near Astor Place, the astral traveler
rebounding eastward, hungry for a fix
on where his yo-yoing and cavalier
crusades are leading him. "Well, there are tricks
and there are tricks," says the unraveler
of Gnostic platitudes. "Then there's the *mind*."
And his so often plays the rarer kind,

XXVIII

the saltimbanque's mnemonic twist, where chance
encounters register as prophesy—
especially in dreams. A furtive glance
across the train; a Greek apostrophe
ensues. "O gentle reader, happenstance
would have you reading a monstrosity
in paperback, called *Junky*—keep your seat."
He lays the bread and salt before her feet.

XXIX

The sonic youth's acoustic solo turn
casts Allen Ginsberg in a beam eclectic
and sublime. Now, as the taciturn
Carl Solomon is gurneyed to electric
diode therapy, our top concern
is Ginsberg's stable passage from the hectic
hour of premonition in the night.
But here comes Dr. Kinsey: *"Ginzo—Light!"*

Canto Eight

The Couch

So, ecce homo.

I
The cartoon features Kat and Mouse, a "brick"
and K-9 law enforcement. *Wow!* The kat's
androgynous! He saunters through the thick
and thin of inky Coconino. Vats
of paper moonlight animate the trick
wherein the feline falls in love with rats.
It's Sunday afternoon and Huncke's reading
comics on the couch. His eyes are bleeding.

II
He doesn't look too good. It's kind of strange—
we thought he'd fallen through the cracks,
and not the ones he rummaged through for change.
But cracks in time. The ones that run like tracks
along the flesh and stone, that rearrange
the Arizona landscape in the stacks
of funny papers. Well, the major domo
of these tales has reappeared. So, *ecce homo.*

III
He relaxes, having howled "asylum!"
in the Greenwich Village warmth of Ginsberg's flat,
continuing his studies in the phylum
Ignatz and the genus *Krazykat*.
His notebooks might be missive bricks. "I pile 'em
in the corner. Well, no time to chat."
And now, in his unconscious state: Ahoy!
Another mouse, another message boy!

IV
The *Zip*-line to a *Pow!* and then the ♥♥♥♥s.
There is no brighter Junkie metaphor
to illustrate the countervailing starts
and fits of Junkydom, the "door"
that fella at the Cafe Wha? imparts
on folk guitar—an entrance to the store
of "curiosities" at "minus zero."
He calls to mind the black cat comic hero.

V

They had a conversation on Minetta
Lane last night, all dialogue balloons
and inky lines. "It isn't a vendetta,"
Dylan said, "just pressure on the goons
in grey." "A switchyard singalong?" "What better
way to improvise?" "...I like cartoons."
Whereat the troubadour said, "Better yet..."
and lit the far end of a cigarette.

VI

And that was it. But Huncke understood
the cryptic line. *The Order of the Rail,*
the silent code, poetic brotherhood.
And sisters, nonetheless—no small detail.
"This scene may have potential, knock on wood."
(Though themes have flamed and smoldered on the trail.)
What matters are the *"L'il Ainjils"* found
wherever something special hits the ground.

VII

Like young Martinez in the methadone
infirmary, the Puerto Rican stud
with perfect manners. Joey is the one
who came by after meds to chew the cud
with Huncke. Joey had about a ton
of soul. "You call me if you need me, Blood."
By "Blood," he meant blood brother. He became
a guiding light. Remember Joey's name.

VIII

And there were others—some were really ghosts—
who murmured in the nightwash on the gang
of drifters underneath the bridge. The hosts
of head-lit saints who prayed in beatnik slang
would almost qualify, in switchyard toasts,
as channels. Maybe you recall the one who sang
the numbers of his own diversity,
the open air his university.

IX

For now, behold the reader in his dream,
narcotic and ecstatic. Narcoleptic,
too, but highly functional. A stream
of neural panels in an apoplectic
yet potential state. A swallowed scream
behind the pancake makeup and the lipstick.
Locked and loaded, ready to explode.
He fades into the final episode.

Canto Nine

The Rape of Manhattan

"Again you catch me while I'm cleaning house."

I

On Christmas Eve in 1968,
three astronauts took ten around the moon.
They read from *Genesis*, and that was great,
and God saw it was good. But all too soon,
the algorithms of the steady state
put fire to the Evinrudes. Balloon
of atmospheric aggie marble blue,
it did us all some good to look at you

II

from outer space. A year of Hell on Earth
resolved in letting pressure from the tire.
The global population shared a hearth
and TV dinner, spinning in the gyre
and waiting for whatever. It seemed worth
the effort to push forward to a fire
on the moon, or on the flat Mojave
(we've been all over that one, Kimosabe).

III

The lunar landing *is* significant—
the last romantic/scientific leap
into the frontier of enlightenment
left trademarks on Tranquility. The heap
of angled rods and engine block we sent
is pasted with the logos. As we sleep
the name of Cracked Air Chemicals will shine
at moonlight's source upon a new design:

IV

The Enterprise. That loose association
linking government, the business suits
and sciences, promotes an escalation
of the skyline. Architecture shoots
in towers north and south through the striation
of the lower atmosphere. Recruits
on Vesey, John and Wall Streets watch in awe.
Chicago and Malaysia declare war,

V

and theirs rise higher. Commercial minarets
that mimic missile silos everywhere!
Petronas, Sears...the global trade begets
The Taipei 101 and Shun Hing Square,
The Tuntex Tower and the Emirates',
a crystallizing urban thoroughfare
in which the rising Enterprise gains traction.
Of course there's art and music in reaction.

VI

"And poetry," says...*yes!* That's *Patti Smith*
in jodhpur slacks and boots. Her ratty T
is quintessential Mapplethorpe. O myth
and mother, middle aged celebrity
of literary metapunk! O kith
of Cale who wowed us with *Piss Factory!*
The Wunderkind and ultra-modern lover
who made a bundle on that Springsteen cover

VII

is the promised headline reader of the night.
Because the night belongs to headlines, pal.
Should I lay off?—A'right, a'right, a'right.
Let's get with Patti's leather protocol—
she lifts her Via Spiga to the light,
its carbon sheen regenerating all
the duotone that we associate
with CBGBs and the Village Gate.

VIII

We're used to atmospheric alterations
in this night of networked memories.
To altered states and lighting variations
on the stage as well. The harmonies
angelic in the wings emit vibrations
of the vatic later 1970s
as Patti strokes the mic stand in the basement.
I think you'd call it theater displacement.

IX

For now, I notice everyone is seated.
Our venue is a downstairs cabaret
affair with candles on the tables. Pleated
crimson curtains back the stage and sway
to backstage ministrations. We are greeted
by a waif in black who makes us pay
a seven-dollar cover. Quite discreet,
this little shakedown on Cornelia Street.

X

And what a Dada theater it is!
Our reader has been jacked above the boards
astride a paper-mache Pegasus.
She holds a scroll, upon which are the words:
*Behold the Seven-Dollar Synthesis
and Alteration.* What, no power chords?
Ah, what the hell is Patti up to now?
But wait—the Poet Morton takes a bow!

XI

Tuxedoed now, entirely in white,
he smiles in painful earnest—apparition
of beneficence. MC: "It's my delight
to welcome a miraculous addition
to our lovely audience tonight—
here's Benoit Mandelbrot, the mathematician!"
Morton gestures lushly toward the back.
Our exit is eclipsed, tuxedo black,

XII

as Mandelbrot is borne into the room
amidst an entourage of academics.
His head looks like a clipper ship in bloom,
its snowy rigging blown in a systemic
pattern through the harbor. Let's assume
the content going forward is endemic
to the forms in nature and their classes.
The great man dons his cardboard 3-D glasses

XIII

and settles slowly in the candle glow,
which spikes a nanomoment as he sits.
Upon the stage, the drafts begin to blow
and toss the virgin sheet, unfolding its
potential to the word and the tableau
of metaphysic drama. To a blitz
of Brahms, the Poet grabs a dangling heel
and climbs up to the flying horse. Unreal.

XIV

Then silence. There's a man upon a chair
at center stage, the aging AWOL sailor,
Huncke. Heightened features of despair
contort his face, a preview or a trailer,
for he shakes his fingers through his hair
and changes his expression. He is paler,
calmer than a corpse as he proceeds
in monologue. "The rose arrangement bleeds

XV

untied and unattended in the river,
vomiting its seeds. Receptive tides
wash inland, counter-current, to deliver
to the heart, on its aortic side,
the fire." "This is pain. I see him shiver,"
says the poet Ginsberg, now beside
the sailor, who again begins to shake.
The chair is bent and banging. It will break!

XVI

"Don't touch him, Carlo, you know what he does."
That's Kerouac, as merchant aquanaut.
"We both do Jack." "You know what happens, Cuz."
But have you noticed there's an astronaut,
or space suit on the chair embossed with "Gus"
across the left lapel? And that it's caught
on fire. Or maybe not. Or is it Huncke
on the chair again, the dying junkie?

XVII

"There you have it" *"Deus ex machina,"*
says Ginsberg. "I'm not buying that today,"
says Jack. "The brother seaman's packin' a
syrette for self control. I look away
and see it coming." "Yes, but Jack, in a
redacted universe..." "That's what you say."
"You thoroughly agree, I've read your files."
The trumpeter upstaging this is Miles.

XVIII

An interlude, a cool interpretation
of *The Order of the Rail* with muted
bell. Perhaps the final variation?
Who can tell? Montana lifts the fluted
cocktail glass, and her participation
is appreciated. She's well-suited
to the role of clubbing ingénue,
Chameleon of the Onyx Rendezvous.

XIX

Tonight the leotard is not in play—
she wears a purple satin robe that drapes
untied to show her satin bustier,
expressionist and black. The shadow shapes
caress her as she sips and pulls away
some satin. We discover how she tapes
her nipples—she deciphers one by Braille.
We see a crimson lacquered fingernail.

XX

"You're sick." "I know it." "Who can help you out?"
That's Ginsberg grilling Huncke on the stage.
Re-enter Kerouac, the roustabout
and rambler of the constant rolling page.
He intervenes by noting that a scout
must always be prepared. A fiery cage
obscures the crimson curtain with a rain
of comets as the shooter finds the vein.

XXI

"Coordinates are in an angry fix,"
says Huncke, "and the constellation too."
"He always talks like this." "Among the tricks
of railway travel"—(Kerouac is through
explaining things). "But Huncke never kicks,"
says Ginsberg. "I know others in the crew
who do. They lecture in divinity."

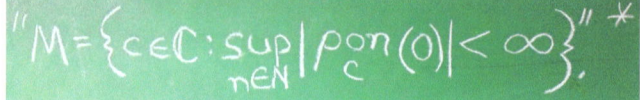

(*Here Huncke quotes the sub-infinity)

XXII

"A geometric layin' of the eight!"—
shouts Poet Morton, leaning on the horse
and Patti in the H-VAC. "*God*, it's late!"
Already shapes are shifting, and of course
the stage is no exception. Contemplate
the crystal props emerging with the force
of rape against the flapping crimson veil.
The leading actor now supports a tail

XXIII

and pimp-rolls on the Deuce between the Times
and 8th on 42nd with a wad
of Benjamins—a throbbing arrow climbs
the ether to the holographic cod-
piece where the mouse has stuffed the dollars. Chimes
and jingles follow him about the odd
and thickly-lined environment: cartoon
and cabaret converged. A thought balloon

XXIV

is clinking quarter notes on whistled halves.
He pushes through the crystals with his fanny
to an office. Everybody laughs
to see the mayor, Rudy Giuliani,
tricked in drag, with frilly-gartered calves.
The mouse is human now, in costume. Can he
control the urge to fiddle with his dipstick?
(The mayor goes so heavy on the lipstick.)

XXV

Oh! He's only reaching for that roll
of hundreds. "Pony up!" says Mickey Mouse.
His money bounces on a ledger scroll.
"Again you catch me while I'm cleaning house,"
is Giuliani's coy reply. The toll
or tithe is pocketed. The mayor's blouse
is loose enough for us to see the tape
he uses underneath *his* cowl and cape.

XXVI

We laugh hysterically. And Mandelbrot
inflates or levitates a bit above
the audience. But then the house is brought
up short by the pounding of a heavy glove
against the on-stage office door. The bought
official gives that plywood prop a shove.
An astronaut is standing in the casement.
A light inside his helmet lights the basement.

XXVII

And now the helmet fills the stage. A flare
behind the crystal visor starts to burn
in violent waves of flame below the square
insignia of CAC. A churn
of carbon smoke surmounts the fire's glare
within the domelike headgear, which in turn
expands, balloonlike, for an instant. When
we see the astronaut in full again,

XXVIII

the suit stands statue-still, its light extinguished.
The mouse and mayor gawk. It's just no good.
The suit, like our heroic proto-linguist,
jerks and drops like any dead thing would
at buckled knees and back. An undistinguished
dance step in the doorway. "Jesus' blood!"
says Giuliani. In a way, that's true.
Resume apocalyptic pas de deux:

XXIX

"I guess one network wasn't good enough
for you." "You're giving up the street." "My friend,
it fits in nicely with the other stuff."
"The sweeps and perp walks, Rudy?" "God forfend!"
They laugh hysterically. "I'm getting tough
on crime!" "By shovin' *Show World*® to *The End*."
"And pricing out the undesirables."
"And hiring certain under-hirables

XXX

to run the law enforcement agencies.
I like your looks—that's just an old expression.
Take it down a notch." "The 'eye that sees'
speaks figurative, Mouse." "Another session
on that sometime, maybe. Papers, please,
the deeds and such" "But wait, I'll call the Hessian
Kerik in to see you out." "I'm sure
I'll find my way without that amateur."

XXXI

An exeunt to fractal atmosphere
and energy across the stage. The set
is struck by greysuit operatives. We hear
the kind of hollow whistling that a jet
produces when its engines fail. A fear,
suspended more than felt, pervades. Forget
the cartoon hologram. It's all too real,
this vision of Manhattan, aerial,

XXXII

within the vectors of the cabaret's
performance space. It's pre-2001
disaster as the sunlit cloud line plays
to the immense baton on Tower One,
its radio antenna. Simpler days?
Or maybe days that ever-faster run
toward a second fulcrum. We're aware
of some impending crisis in the air

XXXIII

or real-time, out-and-out catastrophe
that flies in both directions from Ground Zero
on the line of time. But can one see
a perfect line in nature? I don't know—
Hey, Dr. Mandelbrot...? Eternity
can wait, I guess. The doctor had to go.
His exit leaves us all the more uncertain
of what goes on behind the crimson curtain.

XXXIV

Behold the bright abandoned cabaret
of miracles and code-defying fire.
Of reveries sufficient to the day.
And see the stage, deserted by desire
and treason, twinning masks. Don't look away
from this renowned performance-space-for-hire,
majestic as Chicago's river locks,
as quiet as a mouse's cardboard box.

XXXV

And cut to theater: The Bowery bar
we've been in all along. The poet host
displays the wings of Pegasus—or are
they some wings other? "I propose a toast,"
he says, "To Patti Smith, who's still a star,
to Thurston Moore of Sonic Youth, and most
of all to Gloria, Montana, Moses
and the Stevedore, whose reading shows us

XXXVI

that a first-time reader, one who feels
the heart of the material, can shine.
To cast and crew!" His tribute here reveals
a magnanimity. I redefine
the poet in this context. Morton seals
the Huncke deal. He's managed to combine
the movement with the matters that endure.
"And here's to the eternal raconteur!"...

Canto Ten

Finale

A side of bleeding beef, the Man/Madonna is a Probst portrayal of the Christ.

I
...who dreams of Elsie John, the carnival
hermaphrodite and roadside father/mother
figure in the grey funereal
America (some Midwest town or other),
1931. Before the fall,
but just, his circus summer, working, rather
shilling for that midway heroine
and hero, scoring tea and heroin.

II
He sees the naked bulb above her bed,
her hennaed hair, her clutch of Pekinese.
He sees her body and that egg-shaped head,
remembering her stories. Some of these
have bled into his own. He hears the dead-
bolt crack and cops drop Elsie to her knees,
the weight of hatred reddening their faces.
So many dreams come down to trading places.

III
A side of bleeding beef, the Man/Madonna,
is a Probst portrayal of the Christ,
a haunted traveler, supported on a
railroad crossing signal: *Poltergeist
mit Doppelganger~(Archetype Persona)*.
Mannish boy, he learns the world is priced
to sell. *"The illegitimacy, oh!"*
He speaks of it to those who come and go,

IV
who know the dying man at the hotel.
We're shown the evidence as Super 8
montages navigate the basement's well
of fractured shadows, flaring to create
a backdraft or the aura to a shell
of human flesh reclining in a state
of animate paralysis. The eyes
denote a man relieved of all disguise.

V

It's all a matter, now, of viewing him
in grainy, focus-slipping Kodachrome.
The ossuary walls enhance the thin
proscenium of air on stone, his home
behind a shadow-hacking crowd. A hymn
in video, the credits roll. The Poem.
Another generation on the bum
or trust fund comes. Well, Jesus, let them come,

VI

along with city-born and new-arrival
from Kentucky, Arizona, Maine....
Their journey is a matter of survival
for the Eisenhower-era strain
of street savant, a hope for the archival-
off-the-page and in the urban chain
of elements. We see the speaking ghost
as Huncke plays another kind of host.

VII

The audience begins to mill about
and conversation rises to the level
of a crowded bar. It goes the route
of glad and solemn greetings. Not a revel,
more an Irish wake where the devout
believe the guest of honor beat the devil
clean across an admirable span.
There is hardly even mention of the man

VIII

or mask of death that bites illuminated
dust against the wall and on their backs.
Whose insights and ideas are masticated
in a wordless monologue, the tracks
of which are plaster-cast in desiccated
poetry that molders in the stacks
of storage rooms or echoes in the old
hotel that even now is being sold.

IX

Whose flashing image mouths the words they speak
in this finale, babble though it is.
The first to exit climb the stairs. They sneak,
it seems, like clock-obsessing Judases.
A steady stream develops from this leak,
which leaves The Poet reading Genesis—
with Pegasus's wings, as you'll recall.
His shadow makes an angel on the wall.

X

Did Huncke dream the angel of Martinez?
Perhaps an angel's shadow's apropos.
A guardian from Botticelli's Venus
with the face and fortitude to blow
aside the barriers that curl between us,
determined, single-mindedly, to show
the body peeled and clean. To shell the soul.
I climb through human shadows from the hole.

XI

And up on Bowery, ghosts and angels play
the networks of America at night.
This city on its rivers leans toward day
again. Is Brooklyn hinting at the light?
From the electric street, it's hard to say.
I dog it to the corner, turning right,
engaged with memory and dreams. The Poem.
I'm mumbling in the shadows headed home.

Lost Canto

The Wilderness

"Instead, we set ourselves to work."

I

The moon drops slowly on a battlefield,
a stack of coffins, and a harrowed crowd;
a grayscale meadow where two armies reeled,
the autumn sky one monumental cloud.
A grove where many changes are revealed
in curtain shadows full and fast and loud.
The steady state blows cold and atmospheric
in November's haze of victory-gone-pyrrhic.

II

The tide has turned since bloody Chancellorsville,
though Gettysburg absorbed a lot more blood.
The Rebel yells that once came deadly shrill
choke out in the inevitable flood.
We gather early on a swollen hill
in mourning, in the Pennsylvania mud,
to hear the president's commemoration
preempted by a scalawag oration:

III

"I love the smell of napalm in the morning."
Lincoln, drawn and gaunt, looks down to see
the errant mouse that's known for horning
in on speeches. His prepared apostrophe
has now an antecedent traffic warning
with an ancillary prophesy—
"But nowadays the ghosts get out of line.
We're gonna hafta saw a lot more pine."

IV

"The dead are many, mouse. I understand.
But your vocabulary tries the soul.
This 'Napalm' sounds like some exotic land.
Perhaps the mansion where you make a hole?"
"Not quite. It is the lake of fire canned,
the fist of Revelation. It'll play a role
in World War II. You're on, my brother."
"Wait! World War *II*? You mean there'll be an*other*?"

V

"A couple more, Abe. Then they run together.
Les Militaire Industriel, my friend."
The firmament obliges with some weather
as the sun breaks in and pays a dividend.
New colors stream into the crackled heather
where a face-off toppled on its other end.
"You told me that 'The *Great*' would be "The *Last*.'"
"The future is preamble to the past.

VI

Don't drop your envelope. And keep it short."
The prospect from the boards no longer black-
and-white nor blue-and-greyish, colors sort
themselves in solid fractals with the crack
of an inaudible recurrent theme: *La morte
de l'Amérique.* The stand a catafalque
of gold and purple draperies, the man
embalmed with sorrows... "Fire in the can!"

VII

Or in the hole: A pair of roguish ears
slips through a narrow crack as Abraham
begins the speech. "Four score and seven years..."
But time is relative and on the lam,
complex and military. It appears
and disappears, the war. And Uncle Sam
wants *you*. His call-up rolls without abatement.
"The dead are many" is an understatement.

VIII

That beach in Normandy might be a forest
or an orchard or a stretch of the Pacific;
the merchant sailor a Marine or tourist.
Lightning strikes. The headlines are horrific.
Belligerent, the Empire pays its poorest
citizens to build a monolithic
tidal wall. A hegemonic theme.
The battlefields elide as in a dream.

VIII

In a diner on an upstate lake: The AWOL
Huncke takes his coffee black, regarding
photos taped across a mirror. "They all
locals?" "The departed and the parting.
Service folk." The voice behind the paywall
is the conscience of a great Republic starting
on the long march down. The titan meant
to herald permanent enlightenment

IX

now finds itself some decades in retreat.
"There's not a lot of work up here. The prison
or the army. Do you want something to eat?"
The man beside him makes a small incision
in a western omelet. Huncke slides his seat
a little closer, but the fellow's risen,
leaving Huncke with the steaming plate
of cheesy eggs and toast. "Well, God is great,

X

I guess," says Huncke, reaching for the "57".
But this omelet isn't. Steam keeps bellowing.
It fogs the mirror. Private 1st Class Evan
Jones gawks stiffly as he fades. A yellowing
erasure takes his cohorts out. Eleven
soldiers disappear, the omelet Jello-ing
and jiggling, steams away. A waitress sighs
in helpless empathy. The fry cook fries.

XI

Outside and over Depot Street a cloud
makes metaphor of breakfast, leaking steam.
The western omelet nimbus drapes a shroud
through Penn Yan. Darkness. Dream but not a dream.
It sweeps the local vineyard where a crowd
anticipates a re-enacted stream
of consciousness, a shadow of the war
to end the others that have come before.

XII

The atmospheric bulb portends a crisis
tying Gettysburg and Kaiser to
Afghanistan, Iraq, Al Qaeda, ISIS,
and (let's face it) China. A compromise or two
might stem the tidal wave of Dionysus,
but the downward path runs wider too.
Rhyme-driven, Dionysus may surprise
us with his appetite for apple pies

XIII

at lakeside diners gracing morbid towns
that simmer ghostly on the glacial banks
and vine rows, shelters in the violet downs
where regimental cannon roll in ranks
and angels clad in cobalt fiber gowns
march shotgun to the land of cotton. Yanks.
The sons of dying industry parade
July forth through the intermittent shade

XIV

of wrathful vineyards and a hillside speech
by Frederick Douglas. Oriented North and South,
the Finger Lakes apostrophe will reach
The Friends in Pennsylvania in the pouch
of one "Leviathan." Our angels screech
and sidewind like the severed cottonmouth
through Maryland, a kind of DMZ,
and fall upon the form of our MC,

XV

(Lieutenant?) Morton. "I'm about to light
my third cigar," the errant poet chaws.
"Just sayin'." Well, his eyes lock in a might
too long. A deadpan stare, a horrid pause.
"First rule of fight club, don't forget, is *fight*.
They say smart money's on the Arkin-saws."
His lugging accent begs a painful question.
Let it hang, and deal with the suggestion.

XVI

"I always thought you came from Massachusetts!"
Huncke's joined us, out of uniform.
"Uh, Woburn, as a point of fact, but whose-itz
business?" "...I dunno." "Let me inform
you son: Confucius tells us, if the Fu shits,
wear it. This is what you call 'The Storm.'
A war, bro. Blue or gray, it doesn't matter.
We're all whipped up from the same damn batter."

XVII

"Colors count!" yells Captain Leroi Jones
who rides up with the Negro Cavalry.
"Unfinished business." And outstanding loans?
A debt defining the stark casualty
of our experiment. The voice of Bones
that goads us, redefining liberty
as the essential hole in the Republic.
"The private nightmare always comes up public."

XVIII

"Bound to happen. Let me change my shirt."
"*Same damn batter?* I'll remember that,"
says Jones. "Talkin' that 'smart money' dirt.
The Arkin-saws? You'd better change your hat,
man, while you're at it. Come correct. Avert
sartorial disaster, Morton. Copa-*stat?*"
By that, the hipster gets at "copasetic,"
accent on the "Now." And the synthetic.

XIX

Morton, as an angel robed in Union blue,
unfolds a chessboard and a simple tent.
He puts his glasses on for seeing through
and seats the tall and weary president
who's come unnoticed with his retinue,
the quarrelsome cabinet. A man is sent
to find and escort Lincoln's chess opponent,
a future acolyte and co-deponent.

XX

"That guy looks like Martin Luther King!"
shouts Huncke to a crowd that isn't hip,
coeval, apropos of anything.
No longer hyped to give this scene the slip,
our hero volunteers to wind the spring
and keep the clock and convo at a clip.
The glory of the coming of the Lord
is manifest across the checkered board.

XXI

The pieces roll in visceral contempt
and sepia, in blood and soil, a mix
of mud, a here-and-now, a contretemps
in miniature. Huncke, hungry for a fix
and kinda dying for a break, attempts
to stop the antique clock. The River Styx
erupts and runs beneath a trembling hand
that shakes and hovers over No Man's Land.

XXII

The president attempts to move a piece—
the Union horseman with a golden sword.
Chaos holds his wrist and cuts a crease
into his weathered brow and carves a word
into the cellar of a prayer, a peace
transcending poetry, divine, unheard,
and French. The Reverend King awaits his turn
as Lincoln feels his move begin to burn.

XXIII

The Battle of the Wasteland on the board
lacks something of a sense of geographic
boundaries. We hear nothing like a mystic chord
but something major—Nature in the bathic
sludge of murdered armies, the accord
of blue and grey on black below the traffic
of the burning huevos in the heavens,
to the sky drum laying double on the sevens.

XXIV

Have you ever seen a bayonet run through
the ribcage of a kid whose outsized coat
hangs open from a former rendezvous?
A twilight haze erasing hulks that bloat
into the gulping hills? A silent crew,
pre-choked, 10 fathoms from the sunken boat?
The dagger plunges to its broken hilt
infusing crimson in the meadow silt.

XXV

"America," moans Huncke. "Steady State...."
He stares across the equipoise at Jones
who's pulled a seat up to the game board. "Hate
is a commodity. It's blood and bones
and here you have it." "Guess we gotta wait,"
the hip black captain notes in undertones
regarding Lincoln's hand that hovers still,
suspended by a force against his will.

XXVI

"Non-violence doesn't make a lot of sense."
"But that's the beauty, gentlemen. The doom,
the hallmark of one 'homo sapiens',"
puts Poet Morton. Give that man some room
to swing!—"Historically the present tense
reflects the future perfect like, ka-boom!
The truest poem is the primal scream."
The Reverend stands and turns. "I have a dream...."

XXVII

The optics of his speech, which carries on,
are like an eyeballed echo in reverse.
The poets are his wingmen and the paragon
behind him cuts a marble universe
of human values. Death to Babylon!
Across the battle board there rolls a hearse
with a chimeric horse team front and back.
Its curtained vaults are labeled WHITE and BLACK.

XXVIII
"The *Push-Me-Pull-You* trick!" "You got it, man."
That's Leroi Jones responding to our hero.
"It gets you nowhere," Jones goes on. "The plan
outsmarts itself. It rolls and comes up zero.
See Manassas. Check Afghanistan."
We hear the jagged tones of some far Nero
picking Yankee Doodle mighty fast.
The future is preamble to the past

XXIX
as empires skid like omelets off the griddle,
steaming clouds that complicate the sky
and warm the globe rebounding up the middle,
Fire in the can!, and robot bombs that fly
us to the nub of the eternal riddle:
Israel. "Can't front on that one, guy,"
say Huncke. But Leroi shrugs at the suggestion
that a poet may not ask a simple question.

XXX
Past is prelude, future in reverse.
Now Lincoln stands before the morning crowd
from stanza VI. He's at the second verse:
"We cannot consecrate this ground." A loud
and drawn-out moan erupts. A vatic curse.
"Instead, we set ourselves to work." His shroud
is open at the neck. And now a gust
of wind draws angel's wings. In God we Trust,

XXXI
New Order of the Ages. Cosmic Eye.
Attrition, stalemate in a constant stream;
enlightenment at apex, apple pie;
the dream that's not entirely a dream,
a state like Mississippi and a sky
that bleeds. The ordinary myths apply
to eagles, turkeys and the alligator.
To Dionysus driven by a satyr.

XXXII

"And 'Donald' on the escalator down,"
thinks Huncke, hunkered on a mug of Joe,
but this one at a diner out of town.
He's on the road with Leroi's ghost in tow.
The TV's set on CNN. "This clown
hangs wall-to-wall / He's everywhere we go,"
writes Jones under the moniker *Baraka*.
"Heavy pressure," adds the chessboard clocker.

XXXIII

Outside the diner, sunlight is opaque,
the afternoon oppressive. On the screen
a missile launches. Maybe a mistake?
Or is it last week's or the one between?
"This kid in North Korea takes the cake,
and eats it. Like… a lot," says Huncke. "I mean
vats of chocolate cake!" The ghost is weak,
disconsolate and not inclined to speak.

XXXIV

He's heard a lot of speeches. But the change
and hope they'd promised were a dream deferred,
a forest in a winterscape beneath a range
of Rocky Mountains. Spring is just a word
recurrent in the future tense. It's strange
how the familiar folds to the absurd,
a world dependent on a false construction,
the trick of mutual assured destruction

XXXV

and a state that cannot shake its genocide.
Baraka fades into the steam that rises
from a dozen cups. True spirits glide
into the general malaise that exorcises
a collective sin: communal suicide.
The truth will up, but no one recognizes
flying robots in our present battles.
A gone thing in a Buster Brown box rattles.

Rick Mullin's Huncke
By Paul Christian Stevens
Shit Creek Review, issue 13, 2011—*a review of the first edition*

'This isn't going to be another sonnet', we're told by the last line of *Stanza II, Canto Two* of Rick Mullin's epic in twelve cantos, *Huncke*; and indeed, this poem extends far beyond the ordered but tensioned miniature system of the fourteen-line form. *Huncke* is a huge, sprawling, diverse construction, epically struggling to contain within itself mutually-opposing dynamics which seem to stretch and bend the poem in different directions. And that is one of the things that the poem aims to be, I think: a text which attempts to represent the heterogeneity of contemporary American culture. The critical question is whether such an ambitious intention is matched by the result. This brief review can only point to a few of the elements of the poem's representation of its chosen subject which might address that critical question.

The most obvious element of disparity within *Huncke* is that between content and form. The poem takes its name from Herbert Huncke, who was an icon of the Beat Generation, an American lifestyle and literary movement which valued the anarchic, the spontaneous, the disordered, and the unregimented in reaction against the conformist social values and behaviours of post-World War II America, with its McCarthyite sanctions against free thought and expression, and its short-back-and-sides, man-in-the-grey-flannel suit, lock-step uniformity. In literature, the Beat writers strove to break down received forms, styles and modes, replacing them with attempted spontaneity, free verse, absurdist imagery, cut-up and randomly rearranged non-linear texts, and so forth. Utilising this subversive, anti-establishment character of Herbert Huncke as its focus, Mullin's poem cuts diachronically and synchronically through layers and dimensions of American culture and history. Yet in contrast to its anarchically-oriented subject matter, Mullin's poem has the formal structure of an epic poem in the classical style, divided into traditional cantos, made up of *ottava rima* stanzas, a stanzaic form dating from the late Middle Ages. Here is an immediate dynamic of discrepancy: anarchic, avant-garde anti-formalist material levered uncomfortably (it would seem) into the confines of a conservative, traditional form; and this discrepancy undoubtedly generates much of the abundant electricity and tension of the poem, just as it is emblematic of the tension between heterogeneity and conformity in American cultural history.

Yet I would argue that Mullin's marriage of avant-garde with traditional in *Huncke* is much more complex, and ultimately less incongruous, than this first approximation analysis would suggest. Readers of the poem are signalled from the first few lines that the ostensible formal model for *Huncke* is Byron's comic epic *Don Juan*, and Mullin's choice of intertextuality here is astute, allowing him to achieve the picaresque ambience which I judge to be an important element of his text. But *Huncke* has a less comic, more serious and celebratory major strand as well, and on my reading, the comic element undercuts, arguably a little detrimentally at times, the poem's more serious business.

But let's consider those elements of the *Don Juan* intertextuality which *are* effective. The characters of Don Juan and Herbert Huncke share qualities of the anti-hero; both critique the mores of their respective societies, explicitly and by failing to conform with them. 'If Byron needs a hero, so do I' writes Mullin at the end of his *Canto I*, echoing the opening line of *Don Juan*: 'I want a hero: an uncommon want'. This close allusion clearly and formally establishes the underlying *Huncke/Don Juan* intertextuality; but it does more than this. Hadley J. Mozer has written:

> In announcing his 'want' —i.e., his 'lack' or 'desire'— of and for a hero, Byron is almost certainly parodying several types of early advertising and advertising-related discourse: namely, the newspaper 'want ad' and military recruitment propaganda ... 'I want a hero' is the voice of one crying out in the dailies, the handbills, and the posters of early nineteenth-century England, advertising a poet's 'want' of and for an 'epic' hero, not in the elevated diction of epic, but in the 'vulgar' dialect of advertising— an overture that advertises quite well what the reader can expect from the rest of *Don Juan*, which incorporates numerous languages and just about every kind of jargon and slang that John Bull might have heard spoken in Regency society. And what better way could Byron have possibly begun *Don Juan*, that multi-tongued 'Babel' of an epic poem so full of odd juxtapositions of high and low culture, and so replete with references to the consumer goods and oddities of the age, than to advertise for a hero?*

Mozer's comments illuminate, I think, some key aspects of *Huncke*. Mullin's text, like Byron's, engages with the pop culture and mass media of its era; it too is a "multi-tongued 'Babel' of an epic poem ... full of odd juxtapositions of high and low culture, and ... replete with references to the consumer goods and oddities of the age". In *Huncke*, Americans find their own versions of Byron's consumer goods and oddities: the Internet, FaceBook, Wikipedia, cartoons, punk rock, crazy bohemians, Mickey Mouse, political campaigns, and so forth. However, Mullin's poem takes this field of reference back through various eras of American culture: from 2009, through the 1980s, '60s, '50s, '40s, the American Civil War, the War of

Independence, assembling an appropriately chaotic collage of American iconography in a style which is suggestive of William Burroughs' 'cut-up' technique of narrativisation.

So *Don Juan* is a 'multi-tongued' text, and in that respect it prefigures the modernist and post-modernist heteroglossic narrative mode, which Mullin also deploys to structure his text; much of the significance of *Huncke* is represented through this device. *Huncke's* framing narrative is based on an open-mic poetry reading in tribute to Herbert Huncke held in New York in 2009, but fictionalised for the purposes of the poem; this is an effective context for presenting the various personae that compose a mosaic of vocalisations and perspectives, to enact the representation of the sprawl of American histories and cultures. So we hear the various narratives of open-mic readers, such as the M.C. Morton, (who gives us back-story and context for Herbert Huncke), and a 'white-haired stevedore' who evokes the historic landscape of industrial struggle, and Thurston Moore of Sonic Youth; but spliced into these voicings are many more: we hear Mickey Mouse, Rudy Giuliani, Dr. Kinsey, Benjamin Franklin, Patti Smith, and Allen Ginsberg.

> "It's sketchy, but I do make out a scheme,"
> sings Ginsberg. "Gadgetry no longer hidden
> makes its way up Lexington to ream
> the orifice of human soul. Forbidden
> light, intelligence, and ardour scream
> beneath the rigging of a profit-ridden
> engine (Moloch!) in the stark alliance:
> Government—meet Industry and Science!"
> (*Canto Seven, XIX*)

Yes, that's right—Allen Ginsberg in iambic pentameter *ottava rima*! Moloch indeed! This style of wicked humour based on incongruous juxtaposition is one of *Huncke's* characteristic entertaining elements.

Behind these many voices is the über-voice of the unnamed dominant narrator, who, like the narrator of *Don Juan*, might at the superficial level be taken for the 'poet himself' but who is, in both poems, oddly hard to pin down. In Mullin's poem the narrator slides between 'I' and 'we', at times seeming to represent the poet who has reluctantly attended the tribute, at other times the audience at the tribute, and at other times again some notionally wider, more universal 'we'. This fluidity of narrative identity resembles Australian poet John Tranter's methodology in *The Floor of Heaven*, a poem of similar epic length, scope and importance, which has other points of similarity with *Huncke*, particularly its constantly morphing polyvocality, and its tendency towards a very culturally-specific field of reference. In *The Floor of Heaven* much of the landscape and character typology is as particularly 1950s and '60s bohemian Sydney as Huncke's is New York and America; for the reader unfamiliar with either, this may present some difficulty in parsing the gist, yet in both cases the parsing is well worth the effort.

The dominant (or framing) narrative voice of *Huncke* deploys romantic irony, following its model, *Don Juan*; indeed this is a foregrounded intertextual element. The effect of this romantic irony in both poems is to create a witty, satiric, comic context; after all, the narrator, constantly drawing attention to the fictive nature of his material, and even of 'himself', is inviting us to not take him seriously, to laugh with him at the intrinsic absurdity of roles, events and outcomes. For the purposes of satire in *Don Juan*, I think this mode works effectively indeed; in the case of *Huncke* its effectiveness is less clear-cut, because *Huncke* aims at something much wider than satire, tending to some degree towards a vatic endorsement and celebration of the 'angelheaded hipsters' of Ginsberg, Kerouac, and Burroughs—of whom Herbert Huncke was the prototype. I read *Huncke* as being, although indeed satiric, much more affirmatory of its principal subject matter than *Don Juan*, and in that respect the impact of the *Huncke*-narrator's romantic irony is, I think, a little less certain. But the romantic-ironic voice does help produce the impression of a god-like overview of the very broad sweep of time, place and society painted in both poems.

On the level of formal technique, the apparent lack of seriousness of the narrative über-voice in both *Don Juan* and *Huncke* is further embodied in (amongst other things) the deliberately slap-dash use of rhyme, with forced, macaronic, broken and slant rhymes, in the *improvvisatore* tradition where the author affects a spontaneous carelessness, an aristocratic disdain for the try-hard conscientiousness of more earnest rhymesters. This pell-mell rhyming both creates and is supported by a tone of lazy but exuberant colloquiality. In Byron's poem the attitude embodied is that of the Gentleman rather than the Player—only someone forced to be a professional would bother too much straining to rhyme those damn' verses seriously. Taken together with the romantic irony of narrative, the hit-or-miss rhyming serves to distance narrator and reader from the material, suggesting thereby a more intellectual, less emotionally-engaged stance. It also invokes a sense of poetic instability deriving from the potential wayward randomness of the rhymes. In Mullin's poem the device allows a similar casual and colloquial distancing, and more importantly, creates a ludic effect, an exhilarating joy in the verbal play:

> "There you have it." "*Deus ex machina*,"
> says Ginsberg. "I'm not buying that today,"
> says Jack, "the brother seaman's packin' a
> syrette for self control. I look away
> and see it coming." "Yes, but Jack, in a

>   redacted universe ..." "That's what you say."
>   "You thoroughly agree, I've seen your files."
>   The trumpeter upstaging this is Miles.
>   (*Canto Nine, XVII*)

The rhyme series of '...*Deus ex machina*'/ '...*packin' a*' / '...*Jack, in a*', along with the deliberately imperfect metric scansions of some of the lines, deftly catches the colloquiality of the excited and natural direct speech represented in this stanza. These forced and broken rhymes gesture away from the basic strictures of the poetic form towards the unconstrained free verse that Ginsberg and Kerouac favoured, and contribute much to the satiric and polyvocalic qualities of the poem: within the stanza's eight lines we flip back and forth between the colloquy of Kerouac and Ginsberg, and from them slide to the voicings of Miles Davis' trumpet.

Huncke is, as I said at the beginning of this review, a big poem. It covers a very great deal of cultural and historical ground with an at times bewildering range of allusions, some of which are mainstream and recognisable to the general reader of poetry; others of which seem very specialised indeed. Mandelbrot, Mischianza, Trenton, and Probst, for example, had me scurrying to Wikipedia 'to bone up' as *Canto One, III* would have it.

As is inevitable in such an ambitious piece, some sections will read more strongly than others. I best enjoyed the section in *Canto Six* where Mullin represents some of the painterly denizens of his huge constructed world, and deploys well-executed, vigorous visual imagery in that context. Perhaps Mullin's background in art has made the visual aspect of his work particularly strong, and certainly *Huncke*—in essence a visionary poem—is a poem dominated by visual images, rather than those drawn from the other senses. The dominant visualisations of the work are amplified by Paul Weingarten's very apposite illustrations, which emphasise a kind of hypnotic, dark radiance permeating the book. These verbal and graphic visualisations together evoke a dream-like transitional state, a journey through existential bardos, reminding me somewhat of the filmic style of David Lynch.

It's certainly a very U.S.-American-centric poem, and that will mean some hard work for readers not immersed in the U.S. cultural stream; even for many within it, I imagine. Yet any good poem requires work on the part of the reader, and the residual effect of *Huncke* is a sense of having been enriched by the range of voices and insights that the poem presents, and enriched too by the sharing of a vision, not just of America, not just of the first decade of the 21st century, but of vistas stretching beyond. The reader has moved with that somewhat slippery narrator from his reluctant acceptance of the quest on the dubious imperative of poetry-biz quid-pro-quo ('I'd never been particularly keen / on hipster scribblers, but, you see, I'd sent / out invitations to my own event … '), through a bizarre but remarkable journey towards a more elevated revelation, where 'up on Bowery, ghosts and angels play / the networks of America at night', and where the narrator can ask, 'is Brooklyn hinting at the light?' Despite—because of?—the exigencies of its journey, this odyssey, 'setting sail / across America's agenda' achieves, finally, a visionary luminescence.

This is indeed a very ambitious poem. Full marks to Rick Mullin for attempting it, and for pulling it off so spectacularly. *Huncke* will take its place amongst the more important large-scale works in the American poetic canon.

*('"I Want a Hero": Advertising for an Epic Hero in Don Juan' Hadley J. Mozer in *Studies in Romanticism*, Volume 44, Issue 2, 2005.)

Betcha Can't Read It Just Once
By Siham Karami

A master of the formal modern epic, Rick Mullin's presence in *Huncke* as narrator is more an occasional cameo—no confessionals from this poet, ever—as he weaves, or perhaps I should say architecturally constructs, his multi-leveled tale, which is more a cinematic-cartoon-tech-with-elaborate-pop-ups than a narrative. His formal technique, in all its seemingly unlimited variations, opens spaces where the reader can pause in sheer delight at any random section or stanza, reveling in the wordplay, without knowing what the hell is actually going on. Which is classic Rick Mullin! Mullin is a poet-painter who often chooses cultural or historical topics for epic treatment in classic forms (see, for example, his *The Jones Stones Canzones*; his *Soutine*, a *terza rima* verse narrative about the expressionist painter Chaim Soutine [1893-1943]; or his *Sonnets from the Voyage of the Beagle*, Darwin's fabled ship.) Here he indulges his love of packing in names, places, and events as the building materials of his poem-edifice, loosely tying his hero to the American Revolution, to the moon landing, to World War II, to art history and jazz history, to Mickey Mouse and Rudy Giuliani and Patti Smith, to New York City, of course, and to much more. One need not be on familiar terms with all these specifics to be riveted by this work (though it helps). I myself know comparatively little about the Beat poets or his other cultural/pop references (having entirely bypassed Sonic Youth, although nobody bypasses Ginz), yet the power and thrust of his words drew me in. And I therefore give fair warning to the reader, as in the potato chip commercial, "Betcha can't read it just once."

An epic narrative poem where time is a many-layered thing, *Huncke* is a world-in-a-poem, where its titular hero/anti-hero, inspiration and name-giver to the Beat Poets, and low-life/high-life, infamous, indefinable, freewheeling rebel-without-a-category icon appears in many dimensions: in memory, in history, in the here-and-now, in poetry, in dialogue with "angels" and "ghosts", in holographic animations, in real and fictitious characters of every stripe, all contained within the constraints of a medieval form (*ottava rima* to the cognoscenti) that creates the sense of a forest or a feast of cantos winding their way, stoned-soul fashion, through haunted catacombs or buzzing "red-yellow" honeycombs, an underground world that all begins at a poetry reading attended by Mullin himself.

Upon first reading this poem, you may feel as I did during Shakespearean productions I experienced as a young teen who didn't fully grasp the language but totally loved being in a small theater with all this *Midsummer Night's Dream* craziness going on around me, complete with wild lighting and characters flying in from the ceiling, effects reminiscent of Mullins' verbal techniques in *Huncke*. The crash-pile-up left in my mind after my initial reading created a sense of surprise at how smoothly and sensibly it all began the second time around. Having devoured the whole bag of chips that first time and then come out of the theatre (and it does actually feel like coming out of a theater, or a psychedelic trip), I found myself in something of a cosmic daze from which it took some time to recover—although it *did* have an intermission. (One side effect: speaking in subconscious iambic pentameter.) In this sense, perhaps one can say the poem not only takes its inspiration from Byron's deliberately meandering *Don Juan*, but its cues as well. But then, on second reading, I could be convinced that Mullin's cues are also derived from, of, and about Herbert Huncke himself, including stylistically. To wit, compare this excerpt from Huncke's *Song of Self*...

> I had sent my minute energy quota into the central urge
> aiding each rent in the block of darkness, tugging at each
> fold of light to make way for the one great power: the sun.
>
> And now, as I descended the front steps to the street level—
> the sun was hurling and spiraling across a huge space of blue.

...to this from Mullin's first stanza in *Canto 2*, where Morton is the poet-M.C. at the poetry reading from which this whole drama arises:

> My hope, to plumb the alternate dimension
> I described as arcing from the sun
> in Morton's solar system. My intention—
> reportage. Indulge me if I run
> the gamut such that anyone's attention
> span is taxed, if any episode
> proliferates or breaks a fire code.

It might help to know Mullin is also an accomplished painter and a science reporter, as well as a poet who knows how to mine the elements of his own world and that of his subjects for his art. Thus, he also *paints* this drug-induced sunrise referring to Huncke:

> This he rides at sunrise on the blind.
> A journey toward an easterly injection
> where vermillion hits the ground, a kind
> of natural narcotic or reflection
> of a bleeding eye on Paradise, resigned
> to moaning low and missing its connection.
> *(Canto 3, VI)*

The sense of drama and heightened importance of everything, of an environment that wrenches the reader right out of this world, may be expressed differently, but is intrinsic to both: to Huncke, within the world itself; to Mullin, using Huncke's world and the sheer joy of riffing off such a world while creating alternate universes from more collective memory. Not to be lost here: note that both begin with the sun. Mullin brings in sunrises and sunsets that often seem like metaphors for drugs or their effect on the mind (see above). And both poets combine a uniquely scientific edge with visual acuity. Of course, Huncke became known more for his prolifically weird-and-famous-person-strewn life than his writing, in particular for his inspiration of the more 'successful' Beat poets, and thus he is also the perfect choice for the anti-hero to whom, like Don Juan, strange, often unsavory things keep happening, off-stage.

And Huncke is not only the focal character of this verbal feast, but also its muse. His is the voice in Mullin's head, expressed in *Canto 2, VII*:

> O Delta Jazz! O bottled switchyard red
> that leads to Sterno squeezed through a bandanna!
> O vision of the hero getting head.
> O peeling of the narrative banana.
> The outlaw ambling, crawling through a dead
> end district hoping for one more mañana,
> living it, vicarious, for you.
> The quiet desperation. Working blue.

This "narrative banana" image reappears as we progress. As does the mouse sometimes known as "Mick", and the other guy we still can't seem to get rid of who first appears as a child bugging the hero who, back from a stint in WWII, finds "a kid's been trailing him all afternoon."

> Well, pretty soon
> the punk is offering a light. Reform
> school etiquette—the contrasts are uncanny.
> "So, what's your name, kid?" "Rudy Giuliani."
> *(Canto 4, XVI)*

Despite this surfeit of impressions, one finds meaning and repetitive themes in such a wildly constructed edifice, where what was humorous carries a strangely symbolic sense—like Mickey Mouse with his air of innocence, the sort of Innocence Emily Dickinson would capitalize—and the "poet Morton," who acts as a kind of moderator to Herbert's zany theatrical/circus world, and who finally "managed to combine/the movement with the matters that endure". *(Canto 9, XXXVI)* The third or fourth reading waxes transcendental, especially toward the end, like an eloquent blue moon.

> The future is preamble to the past
>
> as empires skid like omelets off the griddle,
> steaming clouds that complicate the sky
> and warm the globe rebounding up the middle,
> *Fire in the can!*, and robot bombs that fly
> us to nub of the eternal riddle:
> Israel. "Can't front on that one, guy,"
> says Huncke. But Leroi shrugs at the suggestion
> that a poet may not ask a simple question.
> *(The Lost Canto, or The Wilderness, XXIX)*

"Leroi" being Leroi Jones, the poet later known as Amiri Baraka, also known to have sharply criticized Israel, among many other things; just one of the many "loaded" personalities and complex issues that pop up. Not to be forgotten among these are some lesser-known characters such as in *Canto 10, I & II.*

> ...who dreams of Elsie John, the carnival
> hermaphrodite and roadside father/mother
> figure in the grey funereal
> America (some Midwest town or other),
> 1931

...whom cops dropped

>   to her knees,
>   the weight of hatred reddening their faces.

And, before I close, I can't resist mention of this couplet which reveals the energy of facing hard truths with essential optimism which permeates this entire work:

> The truest poem is the primal scream.
> The reverend stands and turns: "I have a dream…"
> *(The Lost Canto, or The Wilderness, XXVI)*

This is clearly not the sort of poetry that "molders in the stacks/ of storage rooms," but the kind that actively creates a world whose ecosystem can't help but stimulate a heightened awareness of the interactions between life, politics, and art, an ecosystem that also contains, for your reading pleasure, a funhouse, where you will definitely get deliriously lost.

About The Author

Rick Mullin's poetry has appeared in various journals and anthologies including *American Arts Quarterly, The New Criterion, Dark Horse, Epiphany, The Raintown Review,* and *Rabbit Ears: TV Poems.* His books include *Soutine* (Dos Madres Press, 2012), *Sonnets from the Voyage of the Beagle* (Dos Madres, 2014), *Transom* (Dos Madres, 2017) and *Lullaby and Wheel* (Kelsay Books, 2019). His chapbooks are *Aquinas Flinched* (Exot Books, 2008), and *The Stones Jones Canzones* (Finishing Line Press, 2012). He is a painter and journalist living in northern New Jersey.

OTHER TITLES AVAILABLE FROM EXOT BOOKS

Schnauzer, David Yezzi ~ 2018
Veil On, Veil Off, John Marcus Powell ~ 2018
A Special Education, Meredith Bergmann ~ 2014
Glorious Babe, John Marcus Powell ~ 2014
Questions, Richard Loranger/Bill Mercer ~ 2013
Turn, Ann Drysdale ~ 2013
Tomorrow & Tomorrow, David Yezzi ~ 2013
Facing The Remains, Tom Merrill ~ 2012
Blue Wins Forever, Paco Brown ~ 2012
They Can Keep The Cinderblock, Mike Lane ~ 2012
Colors, Jay Chollick ~ 2011
Loony Lovers, John Marcus Powell ~ 2011
Filled With Breath: 30 Sonnets by 30 Poets, ed. Mary Meriam ~ 2010
Let Me Be Like Glass, Adriana Scopino ~ 2010
What's That Supposed To Mean, Wendy Videlock ~ 2010
We Internet In Different Voices, Mike Alexander ~ 2009
11 Films, Jane Ormerod ~ 2008
Aquinas Flinched, Rick Mullin ~ 2008
Graceways, Austin MacRae ~ 2008
Prospero At Breakfast, Alan Wickes ~ 2008
Sometime Before The Bell, Ray Pospisil ~ 2006
The Countess Of Flatbroke, Mary Meriam ~ 2006
Blue Glass Cities, Mark Allinson ~ 2006
Prolegomena To An Essay On Satire, R. Nemo Hill ~2006
William Montgomery, Quincy R. Lehr ~ 2006

ORDER ONLINE AT www.exotbooks.com

www.ingramcontent.com/pod-product-compliance
Lightning Source LLC
Chambersburg PA
CBHW041508010526
44118CB00006B/184